This journal belongs to

....

Everyday Bible Promises

FOR WOMEN
JOURNAL

*365 of God's Most
Encouraging Promises*

BARBOUR BOOKS
An Imprint of Barbour Publishing, Inc.

Print ISBN 978-1-68322-344-3

Devotional thoughts and prayers are from *365 Daily Devotions from the Psalms*, *Wisdom from the Bible*, *Whispers of Wisdom for Busy Women*, *Daily Encouragement for Single Women*, and *365 Daily Devotions for Couples* published by Barbour Publishing, Inc.

Scripture quotations marked KJV are taken from the King James Version of the Bible.

Scripture quotations marked NKJV are taken from the New King James Version®. Copyright © 1982 by Thomas Nelson, Inc. Used by permission. All rights reserved.

Scripture quotations marked NIV are taken from the Holy BIBLE, NEW INTERNATIONAL VERSION®. NIV®. Copyright © 1973, 1978, 1984, 2011 by Biblica, Inc.™ Used by permission. All rights reserved worldwide.

Scripture quotations marked NLV are taken from the New Life Version copyright © 1969 and 2003. Used by permission of Barbour Publishing, Inc., Uhrichsville, Ohio, 44683. All rights reserved.

Scripture quotations marked MSG are from *THE MESSAGE*. Copyright © by Eugene H. Peterson 1993, 1994, 1995, 1996, 2000, 2001, 2002. Used by permission of NavPress Publishing Group.

Scripture quotations marked ESV are from The Holy Bible, English Standard Version®, copyright © 2001 by Crossway Bibles, a publishing ministry of Good News Publishers. Used by permission. All rights reserved.

Scripture quotations marked NLT are taken from the *Holy Bible,* New Living Translation copyright© 1996, 2004, 2015 by Tyndale House Foundation. Used by permission of Tyndale House Publishers, Inc. Carol Stream, Illinois 60188. All rights reserved.

Scripture quotations marked NCV are taken from the New Century Version of the Bible, copyright © 2005 by Thomas Nelson, Inc. Used by permission. All rights reserved.

Scripture quotations marked CEV are from the Contemporary English Version, Copyright © 1995 by American Bible Society. Used by permission.

Scripture quotations marked NRSV are taken from the New Revised Standard Version Bible, copyright 1989, Division of Christian Education of the National Council of the Churches of Christ in the United States of America. Used by permission. All rights reserved.

Scripture quotations marked NIRV are taken from the Holy Bible, NEW INTERNATIONAL READER'S VERSION®.Copyright © 1995, 1996, 1998, 2014 by Biblica Inc. ™. All rights reserved throughout the world. Used by permission of Biblica.

Scripture quotations marked NASB are taken from the New American Standard Bible, © 1960, 1962, 1963, 1968, 1971, 1972, 1973, 1975, 1977, 1995 by The Lockman Foundation. Used by permission.

Scripture quotations marked AMP are taken from the Amplified® Bible, © 1954, 1958, 1962, 1964, 1965, 1987 by The Lockman Foundation. Used by permission.

Scripture quotations marked TNIV are taken from the Holy Bible, Today's New International Version®. Copyright © 2001, 2005 by Biblica®. Used by permission of Biblica®. All rights reserved worldwide.

Published by Barbour Books, an imprint of Barbour Publishing, Inc., P.O. Box 719, Uhrichsville, Ohio 44683, www.barbourbooks.com

Our mission is to publish and distribute inspirational products offering exceptional value and biblical encouragement to the masses.

 Member of the
Evangelical Christian
Publishers Association

Printed in China.

INTRODUCTION

And the Scriptures give us hope and encouragement as we wait patiently for God's promises to be fulfilled.

ROMANS 15:4 NLT

This lovely daily devotional journal features themed Bible promises for every day of the year on topics like God's Word, wisdom, faith, prayer, encouragement, love, joy, and more. Listen closely, as each scripture will speak directly to your heart, drawing you ever closer to your heavenly Father. Read and journal on, daughter of the King, and claim His promises every day.

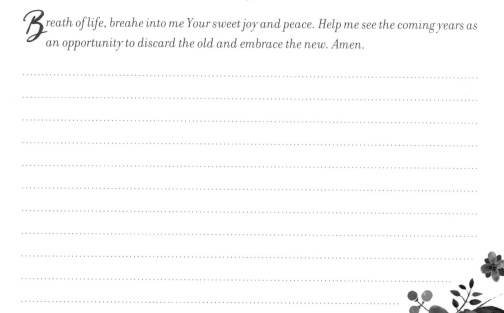

SPIRITUAL REFRESHMENT

For this is what the high and exalted One says—he who lives forever, whose name is holy:
"I live in a high and holy place, but also with the one who is contrite and lowly in spirit,
to revive the spirit of the lowly and to revive the heart of the contrite."

ISAIAH 57:15 NIV

"In six days the LORD made heaven and earth,
and on the seventh day he rested and was refreshed."

EXODUS 31:17 ESV

The giver of life is also the renewer of hope, and He is ready and waiting to fill you with new life, new hope—to transform your heart and lift you out of the pit. All you have to do is ask.

Breath of life, breahe into me Your sweet joy and peace. Help me see the coming years as an opportunity to discard the old and embrace the new. Amen.

Day 2
FAITH

*For it is by grace you have been saved, through faith—and this is not
from yourselves, it is the gift of God—not by works, so that no one can boast.*

EPHESIANS 2:8–9 NIV

*For whatsoever is born of God overcometh the world:
and this is the victory that overcometh the world, even our faith.*

1 JOHN 5:4 KJV

Reason and logic are important traits, but there is something more. Many situations
call for feeling, not just thinking. Faith is like that. It is vital that we learn to think
with our hearts, as well as with our heads.

*Too often, Father, I try to think my way through my problems rather than feeling my
way. Open my heart so that I might know Your love in the deepest way possible. Amen.*

The LORD is my strength, the reason for my song, because he has saved me.
I praise and honor the LORD—he is my God and the God of my ancestors.

EXODUS 15.2 CEV

My voice shalt thou hear in the morning, O LORD; in the
morning will I direct my prayer unto thee, and will look up.

PSALM 5:3 KJV

We need to begin our busy days strong. Not with just a good cup of coffee but some time spent with our source of strength. Taking five minutes or an hour—or more if we're really disciplined—in prayer and Bible reading can make the difference in our day.

Thank You, Lord, for another day. Be my source of strength. In Jesus' blessed name, Amen.

Day 4
WISDOM

Oh, the depth of the riches both of the wisdom and knowledge of God!
How unsearchable are His judgments and His ways past finding out!

ROMANS 11:33 NKJV

The fear of the LORD is the beginning of wisdom:
and the knowledge of the holy is understanding.

PROVERBS 9:10 KJV

Often wisdom comes without great fanfare. It comes to those who wait with open heart and mind. It comes simply and quietly. It comes in the stillness, when God and His Word can get through.

O pen my heart, almighty God. Give me knowledge beyond ordinary knowledge. Teach me more about Your love, Your Word, Jesus the Christ. Amen.

encouragement

For I have sent him to you for this very purpose, that you may know about our circumstances and that he may encourage your hearts.

COLOSSIANS 4:8 NASB

For whatever was written in earlier times was written for our instruction, so that through perseverance and the encouragement of the Scriptures we might have hope.

ROMANS 15:4 NASB

Faith and commitment to God are as challenging today as they were in Bible times. Temptation surrounds us, and even when we obey the Word of God and stand firm, we sometimes grow weak and afraid. But do not fear. Take heart and be strong. You are deeply loved by God!

Dear Lord, thank You for Your love and mercy. Please give me Your peace and strength today. Amen.

Day 6
ETERNITY

"Very truly I tell you, whoever hears my word and believes him who sent me has eternal life and will not be judged but has crossed over from death to life."

JOHN 5:24 NIV

"Only I can tell you the future before it even happens. Everything I plan will come to pass, for I do whatever I wish."

ISAIAH 46:10 NLT

Eternity is now! It starts with the realization that your salvation has granted you a never-ending story—a life without end. Sure, you'll leave this earth at some point, but you'll carry on as a child of God with Him forever and ever.

God, help me to live each day with an eternal focus. Amen.

prayer

Evening, and morning, and at noon, will I pray,
and cry aloud: and he shall hear my voice.

Psalm 55:17 kjv

He will respond to the prayer of the destitute; he will not despise their plea.

Psalm 102:17 niv

Prayer should be a precious thing, since it is communication with our Lord. But how often do we skimp on prayer, pushing it out of our busy lives? Prayerless Christians become weak, helpless believers. But with it we can move mountains.

Lord, sometimes prayer is a last resort as I try to live life on my own power. Renew my prayer life today. Amen.

Day 8
SPIRITUAL GROWTH

Christian brothers, I could not speak to you as to full-grown Christians.
I spoke to you as men who have not obeyed the things you have been
taught. I spoke to you as if you were baby Christians.

1 CORINTHIANS 3:1 NLV

"The seed which fell among the thorns, these are the ones who have heard,
and as they go on their way they are choked with worries and riches
and pleasures of this life, and bring no fruit to maturity."

LUKE 8:14 NASB

Christ never for one minute thought that we should be as perfect as God is. He knew that we are imperfect and sinful. He also knew how much God loves us and wants us to grow and to be happy. With His help we can find joy and maturity.

O Lord, help me to know You, and through knowing You, help me to be like You. Amen.

Whoever of you loves life and desires to see many good days,
keep your tongue from evil and your lips from telling lies.

PSALM 34:12–13 NIV

What you heard from me, keep as the pattern of sound teaching,
with faith and love in Christ Jesus.

2 TIMOTHY 1:13 NIV

A person's words have great power to subtly shift the direction of any conversation, whether encouraging or discouraging. God uses words to guide and encourage His people. With His help, we can do the same.

Father, thank You for the words You've given to show us Your love. Help my conversation to always reflect You. Amen.

Day 10
LOVING OTHERS

This is how we know what love is: Jesus Christ laid down his life for us.
And we ought to lay down our lives for our brothers and sisters.

1 John 3:16 NIV

My dear, dear friends, if God loved us like this, we certainly ought to love each other.
No one has seen God, ever. But if we love one another, God dwells deeply
within us, and his love becomes complete in us—perfect love!

1 John 4:11–12 MSG

One of a Christian's greatest challenges may be to love others. People, after all, are so inconsistent. They cause us pain, even when they don't mean to. Let's face it—loving others can be a real sacrifice. But it's a sacrifice we can't avoid if we want to follow Jesus.

Lord, Your call to love others is so clear. When I struggle, bring Your great love to my mind so that I can love others as You would love them. Amen.

....
....
....
....
....
....
....
....
....
....
....

And Jonathan made David reaffirm his vow of friendship again,
for Jonathan loved David as he loved himself.

1 Samuel 20:17 nlt

Never abandon a friend—either yours or your father's. When disaster strikes,
you won't have to ask your brother for assistance. It's better to go
to a neighbor than to a brother who lives far away.

Proverbs 27:10 nlt

Friendships don't always go smoothly. But even times of disagreement may benefit friends. Perhaps when friendships aren't candy coated, we can be more honest with each other. Let's listen to the courageous love of friends and avoid those who only want to please.

*L*ord, I don't need a bunch of yes-friends. Give me relationships with those who care enough to confront me. I need Your truth in all my friendships. Amen.

Day 12
CREATION

In the beginning God created the heaven and the earth. And the earth was without form, and void; and darkness was upon the face of the deep. And the Spirit of God moved upon the face of the waters. And God said, Let there be light: and there was light.

GENESIS 1:1–3 KJV

One thing I ask from the LORD, this only do I seek: that I may dwell in the house of the LORD all the days of my life, to gaze on the beauty of the LORD and to seek him in his temple.

PSALM 27:4 NIV

Do we seek God's beauty in our environment? Creation points to God's power and awesomeness! Ordinary things draw us into God's presence, where we can praise Him, enjoying His beauty and greatness all the days of our lives.

Magnificent Creator, Your greatness and beauty surround me. May my eyes gaze at You, seeking You, that I may dwell in Your presence continually. Amen.

No one who hopes in you will ever be put to shame,
but shame will come on those who are treacherous without cause.

PSALM 25:3 NIV

I pray that God, the source of hope, will fill you completely with joy and peace
because you trust in him. Then you will overflow with confident
hope through the power of the Holy Spirit.

ROMANS 15:13 NLT

God desires to fill us to the brim with joy and peace. But to receive it, we need to have faith in the God who is trustworthy and who says anything is possible through Him. When you begin to feel discouraged, exhausted, and at the end of your rope, *stop*; go before the throne of grace and recall God's faithfulness.

God of hope, I recount Your faithfulness to me. Please fill me with Your joy and peace, because I believe You are able to accomplish all things. Amen.

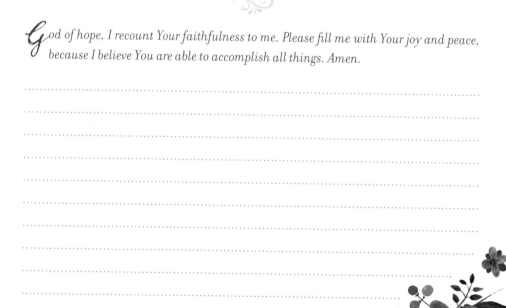

Day 14
WEALTH

As for every man to whom God has given riches and wealth, and given him power to eat of it, to receive his heritage and rejoice in his labor—this is the gift of God.

ECCLESIASTES 5.19 NKJV

Do not wear yourself out to get rich; do not trust your own cleverness. Cast but a glance at riches, and they are gone, for they will surely sprout wings and fly off to the sky like an eagle.

PROVERBS 23:4–5 NIV

Having money and possessions isn't wrong. Even having high-priced possessions isn't wrong. But something is missing when our desire for wealth outweighs our desire for God. We may hold on too tightly to things that don't have eternal value and not cling closely enough to the One who does.

ord, help me to give back to You what You have given to me. Amen.

Consequently, faith comes from hearing the message,
and the message is heard through the word about Christ.

ROMANS 10:17 NIV

And Peter answered him and said, Lord, if it be thou, bid me come unto thee
on the water. And he said, Come. And when Peter was come down
out of the ship, he walked on the water, to go to Jesus.

MATTHEW 14:28–29 KJV

To the skeptic, logic must pervade every situation. But to the person of faith, logic gives way to faith. Even when our prayers remain unanswered, we continue to pray. Even when God is silent, we continue to believe. And though we grope for answers, we continue to trust. In all situations, God asks us to hold fast to our faith.

D *ear Lord, please forgive me for allowing my problems to undermine my faith. I trust*
You, knowing that my faith in You is never futile. Amen.

Day 16
HELPING OTHERS

Now we who are strong [in our convictions and faith] ought to [patiently] put up with the weakness of those who are not strong, and not just please ourselves.

ROMANS 15:1 AMP

Yet it was good of you to share in my troubles. Moreover, as you Philippians know, in the early days of your acquaintance with the gospel, when I set out from Macedonia, not one church shared with me in the matter of giving and receiving, except you only.

PHILIPPIANS 4:14–15 NIV

As our lives become more hectic and crowded, finding a way to help others—and be helped by them—can open the door to blessings for everyone, including more time with our family and friends, and more rest for our minds, bodies, and souls. God never meant for us to face our days alone.

Father God, You have brought so many good people into my life. Help me remember to offer my help to them and to ask for help when I need it. Amen.

....
....
....
....
....
....
....
....
....

He himself bore our sins in his body on the tree, that we might die to sin and live to righteousness. By his wounds you have been healed.

1 PETER 2:24 ESV

The next day he saw Jesus coming toward him, and said, "Behold, the Lamb of God, who takes away the sin of the world!"

JOHN 1:29 ESV

The wages of sin is death. A wise person avoids life-threatening situations at any cost. That is what we should do as Christians. We should do everything in our power to avoid sin, which should be as odious to us as death itself.

L ord God, I want my life to be pleasing to You. Guide me through the power of Your Holy Spirit. Amen.

Day 18
CONTENTMENT

You make my life pleasant, and my future is bright.

PSALM 16:6 CEV

But godliness with contentment is great gain.

1 TIMOTHY 6:6 KJV

How can we learn to be content? We must start looking to Jesus. If we take hold of all we have as joint heirs with Christ and as partakers of grace, we will have no desire for the world's riches. We need a fresh vision for who we are in Christ. Therein we will find contentment.

Father, I am so foolish. I have everything in You, yet I try to find more in the world and in myself. Thank You for the true riches I have found through Jesus Christ. Amen.

The path of lazy people is overgrown with briers;
the diligent walk down a smooth road.

PROVERBS 15:19 MSG

No matter how much you want, laziness won't help a bit,
but hard work will reward you with more than enough.

PROVERBS 13:4 CEV

The Bible gives us a simple solution to conquer the sin of sloth. Namely, God admonishes us to do our best in whatever task we undertake, no matter how large or menial the job. As we give our best, God returns the gesture. He blesses us with a centered life and a more meaningful, productive existence.

Dear Jesus, please forgive me for the times I have been lazy. Empower and remind me to give my best in everything I do, just as You give Your best to me. Amen.

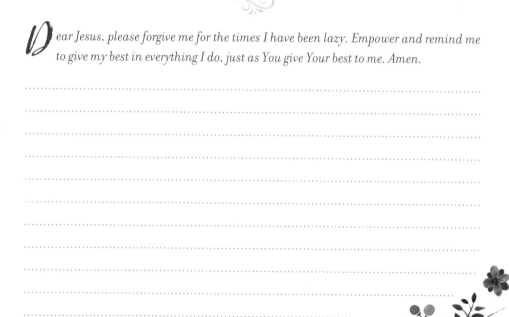

Day 20
REST

. . . .

"Consider the lilies of the field, how they grow: they neither toil nor spin."
MATTHEW 6:28 NKJV

I will both lay me down in peace, and sleep:
for thou, LORD, only makest me dwell in safety.
PSALM 4:8 KJV

Don't let the thoughts of days past and future keep you from catching those forty winks. Fall asleep in God's Word, rest easy, and rise refreshed.

God, with Your Word in my thoughts, I can lie down in peace and sleep. You will keep me safe, now and forever, as I rest and then rise in Your power. Amen.

. . . .

Therefore, since we have been justified by faith,
we have peace with God through our Lord Jesus Christ.

ROMANS 5:1 ESV

For to us a child is born, to us a son is given, and the government will be
on his shoulders. And he will be called Wonderful Counselor,
Mighty God, Everlasting Father, Prince of Peace.

ISAIAH 9:6 NIV

Peace with God does not always mean a calm time of happiness. The salvation that Jesus brought comes with a price: conflict against evil. But in the end, all who trust in Him experience the peace of eternal life.

*W*hile life on earth may be rocky, Lord, nothing can upset the peace I have found in You. Amen.

. . . .
. . . .
. . . .
. . . .
. . . .
. . . .
. . . .
. . . .
. . . .
. . . .
. . . .
. . . .

Day 22
PERSEVERANCE

Ask and keep on asking and it will be given to you; seek and keep on seeking and you will find; knock and keep on knocking and the door will be opened to you.

MATTHEW 7:7 AMP

For if we are faithful to the end, trusting God just as firmly as when we first believed, we will share in all that belongs to Christ.

HEBREWS 3:14 NLT

God calls for persistence, also known as perseverance, over a dozen times in the New Testament. He means for the trials that come our way to increase our perseverance. When we successfully pass small hurdles, He may put bigger ones in our way. Why? Because He loves us. Persistence results in faith that is pure, molten gold.

Lord, we can only persist because You are unchanging. We pray that we will keep our eyes fixed on You and keep moving forward. Amen.

*"See now that I myself am he! There is no god besides me. I put to death and I bring
to life, I have wounded and I will heal, and no one can deliver out of my hand."*

DEUTERONOMY 32:39 NIV

*Let all that I am praise the LORD; may I never forget the good things he does for me.
He forgives all my sins and heals all my diseases.*

PSALM 103:2–3 NLT

Our heavenly Father patiently waits for us to come to Him with the fragments of our
shattered lives. When we bring our brokenness to the foot of the cross, He provides
a life-giving transfusion, healing the hurt and shaping His children into healthy,
whole vessels.

*L ord, I bring my shattered remnants and broken dreams to You. Bring healing and
wholeness to my life. Amen.*

Day 24
GOD'S LOVE

. . . .

*"For God so loved the world that He gave His only begotten Son,
that whoever believes in Him should not perish but have everlasting life."*

JOHN 3:16 NKJV

*"Understand, therefore, that the LORD your God is indeed God. He is the faithful God
who keeps his covenant for a thousand generations and lavishes his
unfailing love on those who love him and obey his commands."*

DEUTERONOMY 7:9 NLT

Many things in life are pricey. Name-brand clothing, cars—even phones. But they will
wear out or be used up before long, no matter what the price tag. By contrast, God's
preserving, unfailing love is priceless. His amazing love was costly, but it's not pricey.

*T*hank You, Father, that no price tag can be put on Your lavish love for me. Amen.

. . . .
. . . .
. . . .
. . . .
. . . .
. . . .
. . . .
. . . .
. . . .
. . . .
. . . .
. . . .

Does not the potter have the right to make out of the same lump of clay some pottery for special purposes and some for common use?

ROMANS 9:21 NIV

God has set up his kingdom in heaven, and he rules the whole creation.

PSALM 103:19 CEV

God has created a glorious world, and He has freely given it to us. The early quiet of the day is a beautiful time to encounter the Lord. Give Him your early hours, and He will give you all the blessings you can hold.

I raise my voice to You in the morning, Lord. Help me to appreciate Your new day, and use it to the fullest. Amen.

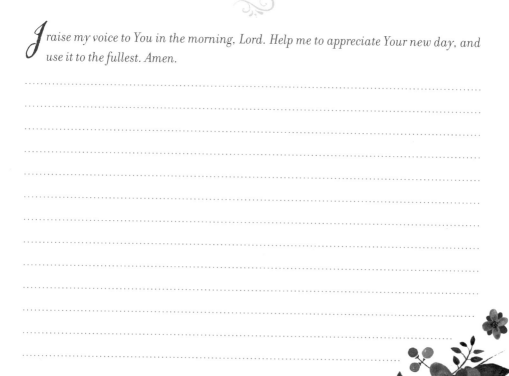

Day 26
TRIALS

Consider it a sheer gift, friends, when tests and challenges come at you from all sides.

JAMES 1:2 MSG

Weeping may endure for a night, but joy cometh in the morning.

PSALM 30:5 KJV

Some trials are short lived. Others are more complex. As believers, we can find joy in the Lord even as certain trials remain a backdrop in our lives. Your loving heavenly Father has not forgotten you. You may feel that relief will never come, but take courage. It will.

God, where there is anguish in my life, may Your joy enter in. I ask for grace to face my trials, knowing that in time You will replace weeping with joy. Amen.

*If anyone is confident that he is Christ's, he should reflect
and consider this, that just as he is Christ's, so too are we.*

2 CORINTHIANS 10:7 AMP

*If you're abused because of Christ, count yourself fortunate. It's the Spirit of God and
his glory in you that brought you to the notice of others. If they're on you because you
broke the law or disturbed the peace, that's a different matter. But if it's because
you're a Christian. . .be proud of the distinguished status reflected in that name!*

1 PETER 4:14–16 MSG

When you gave your heart to God, His light came on inside you. Your life should
reflect the character and nature of the One who created you. As you point others
to God, your light shines, repelling darkness and giving comfort to everyone God
brings across your path.

J esus, show me what I can do and say to let my light shine brightly. Amen.

Day 28
FALSE TEACHING

Then the LORD said to me, "The prophets are prophesying falsehood in My name. . . .
They are prophesying to you a false vision. . .Therefore thus says the LORD concerning
the prophets. . .although it was not I who sent them—yet they keep saying,
'There will be no sword or famine in this land'—by sword
and famine those prophets shall meet their end!"

JEREMIAH 14:14–15 NASB

For of this sort are they which creep into houses, and lead captive silly women
laden with sins, led away with divers lusts, ever learning,
and never able to come to the knowledge of the truth.

2 TIMOTHY 3:6–7 KJV

We are silly when we are so open-minded that we believe things we know are too
good to be true—a slick sales pitch, or the unexamined claims of someone offering
us something larger, better, or easier. If we are to be truly strong, we must listen to
God alone.

Father, I have been confused by many voices in this world. Open my ears to Your voice
alone. Settle my heart in Your Word. Amen.

GOD'S PROMISES

I have ruled this way, and God will never break his promise to me. God's promise is complete and unchanging; he will always help me and give me what I hope for.

2 SAMUEL 23:5 CEV

In hope of eternal life which God, who cannot lie, promised before time began.

TITUS 1:2 NKJV

God always keeps His word. The Bible is filled with the promises of God—vows to us that we can trust will be completed. God never lies. Lying is not in Him. He sees us as worthy of His commitment.

God, thank You that Your Word is trustworthy and true. Praise You for Your many promises. Amen.

Day 30
GOD'S PRESENCE

Know therefore this day, and consider it in thine heart, that the Lord he is God in heaven above, and upon the earth beneath: there is none else.

DEUTERONOMY 4:39 KJV

And he said, My presence shall go with thee, and I will give thee rest.

EXODUS 33:14 KJV

It is not so important that we feel God's presence with us as it is that we have faith in His being with us always. Feelings come and go, but the presence of God in our lives never changes.

et me sense Your loving arms around me, Lord; but when I don't, help me to remember that You are there, anyway. Amen.

LAUGHTER

"He will yet fill your mouth with laughter, and your lips with shouting."

JOB 8:21 ESV

All you saints! Sing your hearts out to GOD! Thank him to his face! He gets angry once in a while, but across a lifetime there is only love. The nights of crying your eyes out give way to days of laughter.

PSALM 30:4–5 MSG

When Satan bombards us with lies—"God's not real"; "You'll never get that job"; "You're unlovable"—it's time to look back to God's Word. Imbed in your mind the truth that with God, nothing is impossible. And then, in the midst of the storm, laugh, letting the joy of God's truth be your strength.

I trust in Your Word, Lord. Help me to rest in that assurance. Amen.

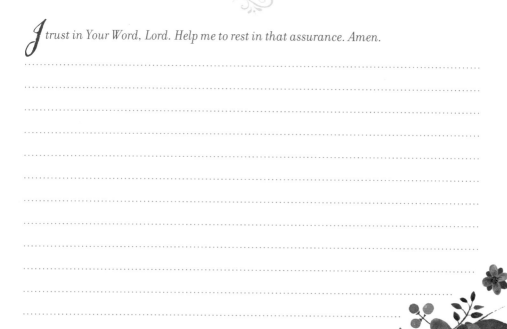

Day 32
CHRISTIAN LIFE

Christian brothers, we ask you, because of the Lord Jesus, to keep on living in a way that will please God. I have already told you how to grow in the Christian life.

1 THESSALONIANS 4:1 NLV

He found Saul and brought him to Antioch, where they met with the church for a whole year and taught many of its people. There in Antioch the Lord's followers were first called Christians.

ACTS 11:26 CEV

As hard as we might try to live as God would want, we find that we can't quite do it. We need help. God gives us that help if we only seek it. Prayer, scripture, and the support of fellow believers makes living the Christian life much easier and more fulfilling.

W hen I struggle with life, Lord, grant me Your wisdom to lead me through. Amen.

....
....
....
....
....
....
....
....
....
....
....
....

For this they willfully forget: that by the word of God the heavens were of old, and the earth standing out of water and in the water, by which the world that then existed perished, being flooded with water.

2 PETER 3:5–6 NKJV

The Word was first, the Word present to God, God present to the Word. The Word was God, in readiness for God from day one.

JOHN 1:1–2 MSG

Without God's Word, how would we know about God? God's Word helps us know Jesus, whom the Bible also calls the Word. Through the written Word and His Son, God has shown us the way to Himself.

Lord, let me see You through Your Word. My desire is to know You more every day. Amen.

Day 34
DECISION MAKING

The path of right-living people is level. The Leveler evens the road for the right-living. We're in no hurry, God. We're content to linger in the path sign-posted with your decisions.

ISAIAH 26:7–8 MSG

I press on to reach the end of the race and receive the heavenly prize for which God, through Christ Jesus, is calling us.

PHILIPPIANS 3:14 NLT

As humans, we often want to cover our bases, assuring ourselves that our decisions are right, but we must not lose ourselves in the analysis. Find your strength in the leadership of the Holy Spirit and move forward with confidence.

Lord, help me to trust You in the decisions I make throughout my day. Help me to stop second-guessing myself and trust who You created me to be. Amen.

*I tell you that any sinful thing you do or say can be forgiven. Even if you speak
against the Son of Man, you can be forgiven. But if you speak against the Holy Spirit,
you can never be forgiven, either in this life or in the life to come.*

MATTHEW 12:31–32 CEV

*"If you then, being evil, know how to give good gifts to your children, how much more
will your heavenly Father give the Holy Spirit to those who ask Him?"*

LUKE 11:13 NASB

Christ died to heal our relationship with God, but the Holy Spirit enables us to live for
Him. Our relationship is with the Father, Son, and Holy Spirit, and in our lives, each
works in concert with the other persons of the Trinity.

*ord, without Your Holy Spirit helping me, I would never be able to live for You. Thank
You! Amen.*

Day 36
WEALTH

I have seen another evil under the sun, and it weighs heavily on mankind:
God gives some people wealth, possessions and honor, so that they lack nothing
their hearts desire, but God does not grant them the ability to enjoy them,
and strangers enjoy them instead. This is meaningless, a grievous evil.

ECCLESIASTES 6:1–2 NIV

"Sell your possessions and give to those in need. This will store up treasure
for you in heaven! And the purses of heaven never get old or develop holes.
Your treasure will be safe; no thief can steal it and no moth can destroy it."

LUKE 12:33 NLT

Though possessions are gifts from God, they can also distract believers from the fact that all in this life is temporary. However many possessions God gives us, we need to share them generously and store up treasures in heaven.

*H*eavenly Father, keep my possessions from becoming my focus. I have been blessed with many things; help me to share them with others. Amen.

....

....

....

....

....

....

....

....

FORGIVENESS

Who is a God like you, who pardons sin and forgives the transgression of the remnant of his inheritance? You do not stay angry forever but delight to show mercy. You will again have compassion on us; you will tread our sins underfoot and hurl all our iniquities into the depths of the sea.

MICAH 7:18–19 NIV

But if ye do not forgive, neither will your Father which is in heaven forgive your trespasses.

MARK 11:26 KJV

When we knowingly sin against God, we're often hesitant to seek His face for forgiveness. Even in those rare instances when we sin in ignorance, we must still humble ourselves before Him. But we never need fear that He'll turn away from us. Such total forgiveness should bring us running back to Him on a daily basis.

Heavenly Father, forgive me for both secret and presumptuous sins. Help me to live faithfully. Amen.

Day 38
GOD'S FAITHFULNESS

. . . .

And we know that all things work together for good to them that love God,
to them who are the called according to his purpose.

ROMANS 8:28 KJV

"I will not leave you as orphans; I will come to you."

JOHN 14:18 NIV

God never, ever abandons us. No matter how busy we are, He never forgets us. He promised His followers that He would always help and support them, a promise He still keeps today.

Lord, You sent Your Holy Spirit as a helper and guide. No matter how tough our world becomes, let us remember Your presence in our lives. Amen.

His lord said unto him, Well done, thou good and faithful servant: thou hast been faithful over a few things, I will make thee ruler over many things: enter thou into the joy of thy lord.

MATTHEW 25:21 KJV

Though you have not seen him, you love him; and even though you do not see him now, you believe in him and are filled with an inexpressible and glorious joy, for you are receiving the end result of your faith, the salvation of your souls.

1 PETER 1:8–9 NIV

God's joy isn't based on our circumstances; rather, its roots begin with the seed of God's Word planted in our hearts. Suddenly, our hearts spill over with joy, knowing that God loves us and that He has complete control of our lives. Joy is Jesus.

D ear Jesus, knowing You surpasses anything and everything else the world offers. Never allow the joy in my heart to evaporate in the desert of difficulties. Amen.

Day 40
EVIL

. . . .

The Lord is watching everywhere, keeping his eye on both the evil and the good.

PROVERBS 15:3 NLT

*And He was saying, "That which proceeds out of the man, that is what defiles
the man. For from within, out of the heart of men, proceed the evil thoughts."*

MARK 7:20–21 NASB

Evil people are not to be hated, but pitied. They are our mission in life. Lives devoid
of the good news are lives not worth living. Reach out to people who do wrong through
your prayers. They need them most of all.

*ord, show me how to love even the most unlovable people. Instead of anger, let me show
compassion. Fill my heart with a love that will overcome evil. Amen.*

I have no greater joy than to hear that my children walk in truth.

3 JOHN 1:4 KJV

And again, I will put my trust in him. And again,
Behold I and the children which God hath given me.

HEBREWS 2:13 KJV

How can our children learn to be quiet and meditate on God's Word when their schedules are hectic and every minute is committed? It's easy to crowd out the things that matter most to God: worshiping Him, listening to Him, and seeking His presence.

Heavenly Father, as my children grow up, I pray they will learn not just how to stay busy but how to stay still. And within that stillness to hear Your quiet voice. Amen.

Day 42
FORGIVENESS

For thou, Lord, art good, and ready to forgive;
and plenteous in mercy unto all them that call upon thee.

PSALM 86:5 KJV

"They refused to listen and failed to remember the miracles you performed among
them. They became stiff-necked and in their rebellion appointed a leader in order
to return to their slavery. But you are a forgiving God, gracious and compassionate,
slow to anger and abounding in love. Therefore you did not desert them."

NEHEMIAH 9:17 NIV

The Lord desires for us to have relationships founded on kindness, tenderheartedness, and forgiveness. As we, through the Holy Spirit in us, are able to live this kind of life, we model Christ to others. Our purpose in life is to become more like Him. Why not begin living a life of forgiveness today?

Forgiving Lord, I desire to be more like You. Enable me to forgive those who have hurt me
and to live a life of forgiveness. Amen.

Pray in the Spirit at all times and on every occasion.
Stay alert and be persistent in your prayers for all believers everywhere.

Ephesians 6:18 NLT

I want everyone everywhere to lift innocent hands toward heaven and pray,
without being angry or arguing with each other.

1 Timothy 2:8 CEV

Nothing draws us closer to other people than praying for them. Asking for God's intervention in their lives is an awesome privilege. We experience matchless rejoicing when our prayers are answered. Let's not just promise to pray for someone. Let's be faithful to do it!

Dear Lord, often I have good intentions to pray for others but fail to follow through.
Help me to be faithful in prayer so that I may see Your power at work. Amen.

Day 44
TRUTH

God can't stomach liars; he loves the company of those who keep their word.

PROVERBS 12:22 MSG

If you do the right thing, honesty will be your guide. But if you are crooked, you will be trapped by your own dishonesty.

PROVERBS 11:3 CEV

When we are honest, we take hold of the truth of Christ and spread it to others we meet. It is by living honest, straightforward lives that we move closer to God in all His glory.

I wish that I could be the person You want me to be, almighty God. Empower me with the spirit of truth, that I might always live honestly and openly in Your sight. Amen.

"You have six days each week for your ordinary work, but the seventh day is a Sabbath day of rest dedicated to the LORD your God. On that day no one in your household may do any work."

EXODUS 20:9–10 NLT

"Be strong and courageous, and do the work. Don't be afraid or discouraged, for the LORD God, my God, is with you. He will not fail you or forsake you."

1 CHRONICLES 28:20 NLT

Are you feeling disheartened by the sheer size of your responsibilities? Be strong and courageous! Do the work! Don't be afraid or discouraged by the size of the task. The Lord God is with you, and He will not fail or forsake you!

Dear Lord, give me strength and courage to do the work You have called me to do. Take away my fear and discouragement, and help me to lean on You. Amen.

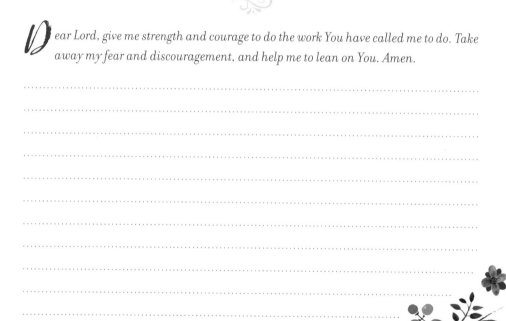

Day 46
FRIENDSHIP

And he said unto them, Which of you shall have a friend, and shall go unto him at midnight, and say unto him, Friend, lend me three loaves; for a friend of mine in his journey is come to me, and I have nothing to set before him? And he from within shall answer and say, Trouble me not: the door is now shut, and my children are with me in bed; I cannot rise and give thee. I say unto you, Though he will not rise and give him, because he is his friend, yet because of his importunity he will rise and give him as many as he needeth.

LUKE 11:5–8 KJV

The righteous choose their friends carefully, but the way of the wicked leads them astray.

PROVERBS 12:26 NIV

Some friends are not worth having: the kind who deceive us and lead us astray. Friendships should sharpen faith, not destroy it.

*F*ather, open my eyes to the damaging friendships in my life. Let nothing harm my relationship with You. Amen.

....
....
....
....
....
....
....
....
....
....

* *

Anxiety in the heart of man causes depression, but a good word makes it glad.

Proverbs 12:25 nkjv

Without the help of the Lord it is useless to build a home or to guard a city.
It is useless to get up early and stay up late in order to earn a living.
God takes care of his own, even while they sleep.

Psalm 127:1–2 cev

Stress can make you feel like a grape in a winepress. The good news is that God has given you everything you need, but it's up to you to utilize the wisdom He has provided. Alleviate pressure where you can and then know that God's power will make up for the rest.

ord, help me to do what I can do; and I'll trust You to do for me those things that I can't do. Amen.

....
....
....
....
....
....
....
....
....
....
....
....

Day 48
GOD'S LOVE

"The Lord your God is with you, the Mighty Warrior who saves. He will take great delight in you; in his love he will no longer rebuke you, but will rejoice over you with singing."

ZEPHANIAH 3:17 NIV

"For the Father Himself loves you, because you have loved Me and have believed that I came forth from the Father."

JOHN 16:27 NASB

Those who are lucky enough to find someone to share their lives with enjoy a special gift from God. But for every person, the love of God is very real, and very much freely given. We can be happy because we know we are loved.

O Lord, giver of life and giver of love, though I am unworthy, I thank You for loving me so much. Help me to know Your love at all times. Amen.

Shout for joy, you heavens; rejoice, you earth; burst into song, you mountains!
For the Lord comforts his people and will have compassion on his afflicted ones.

ISAIAH 49:13 NIV

In the multitude of my thoughts within me thy comforts delight my soul.

PSALM 94:19 KJV

The world hardly knows the meaning of comfort. But the Spirit of God offers the best there is to have. When we come to Him in pain and faith, He touches our hearts in tender ways that no human can. He offers a shoulder to cry on.

Thank You, heavenly Father, for Your loving care. Comfort me when I hurt, I pray. Amen.

Day 50
GUILT

*If we confess our sins, he is faithful and just to forgive us our sins,
and to cleanse us from all unrighteousness.*

1 John 1.9 kjv

*Let the wicked forsake his way, and the unrighteous man his thoughts:
and let him return unto the Lord, and he will have mercy upon him;
and to our God, for he will abundantly pardon.*

Isaiah 55:7 kjv

Ask forgiveness from the Lord, receive it, and move forward in the glory of God's grace. You sins are forgiven, indeed!

Cleanse me and prepare me for the wonderful life that is to come, Jesus. May I learn from my mistakes and grow from them without allowing them to control my life. Amen.

"But as for you, be strong and do not give up, for your work will be rewarded."

2 CHRONICLES 15:7 NIV

"The LORD repay your work, and a full reward be given you by the LORD God of Israel, under whose wings you have come for refuge."

RUTH 2:12 NKJV

God has given each of us work to do. Sometimes the labor is new and exciting. Sometimes the job is repetitive. Both types are given to us for His purpose. We can look forward to the reward God has for us when we complete the tasks He has set before us.

Thank You, Lord, for the work I can do. Give me joy as I serve. Amen.

Day 52
WORDS

"And these words that I command you today shall be on your heart."

DEUTERONOMY 6:6 ESV

The words of the LORD are pure words; as silver tried
in a furnace on the earth, refined seven times.

PSALM 12:6 NASB

We've all experienced moments when words are out of our mouths before we know it. If we would stop and think before speaking, we wouldn't hurt the feelings of others as often as we do. Weigh your words carefully before using them. And if you've said something you cannot take back, be quick to ask forgiveness.

Dear Lord, I want to glorify You and edify others, not cut them down. Help me to think before I speak, and may my words be filled with compassion and love. Amen.

There will be no more night. They will not need the light of a lamp or the light of the sun, for the Lord God will give them light. And they will reign for ever and ever.

REVELATION 22:5 NIV

And God called the expanse Heaven. And there was evening and there was morning, the second day.

GENESIS 1:8 ESV

Christ Himself spent a good deal of His life preparing for His ministry and work. Like Him, we are growing, maturing, and preparing for the kingdom of God, which awaits us. We are being made ready for our heavenly home.

Lord, create in me a real hunger for Your truth that I may be more like You here on earth and forever in heaven. Amen.

Day 54
DOUBT

. . . .

"Truly I tell you, if anyone says to this mountain, 'Go, throw yourself into the sea,' and does not doubt in their heart but believes that what they say will happen, it will be done for them."

MARK 11:23 NIV

If any of you lacks wisdom, you should ask God, who gives generously to all without finding fault, and it will be given to you. But when you ask, you must believe and not doubt, because the one who doubts is like a wave of the sea, blown and tossed by the wind.

JAMES 1:5–6 NIV

It's good to know that God is there for us when we turn to Him with our doubts and questions. When we find ourselves faced with new and different beliefs, it is wise to take them to God in prayer.

God, I think that I know what to believe, but new things come up almost every day. Help me to sort out what is right and good to believe. Amen.

. . . .
. . . .
. . . .
. . . .
. . . .
. . . .
. . . .
. . . .
. . . .

God will speak to this people, to whom he said, "This is the resting place, let the weary rest"; and, "This is the place of repose"—but they would not listen.

ISAIAH 28:11–12 TNIV

For thus saith the Lord GOD, the Holy One of Israel; In returning and rest shall ye be saved; in quietness and in confidence shall be your strength: and ye would not.

ISAIAH 30:15 KJV

We are called to be God's workers, His hands and feet in this world. But we are also called to rest and pray. Jesus put a priority on this, frequently leaving the crowd to seek solitude. Make time to rest. Find a place that is quiet where you can pray. Jesus modeled this for us. He wants us to find rest in Him.

Father, show me the importance of rest. Allow me to say no to something today in order that I might say yes to some quiet time with You. Amen.

Day 56
MOTIVES

. . . .

We justify our actions by appearances; GOD examines our motives.

PROVERBS 21:2 MSG

People may be pure in their own eyes, but the LORD examines their motives.

PROVERBS 16:2 NLT

The Lord examines the motives of the heart. That can be both a blessing and a challenge. We all make mistakes, so errors made with a pure motive will be seen as such. However, good actions made with an impure motive will not be rewarded.

Heavenly Father, forgive me for the dishonesty behind impure motives. Thank You for leading me into all truth. Amen.

. . . .

. . . .

. . . .

. . . .

. . . .

. . . .

. . . .

. . . .

. . . .

. . . .

. . . .

. . . .

SHARING THE GOSPEL

Also pray for us that God will give us an opportunity to tell people his message.
Pray that we can preach the secret that God has made known
about Christ. This is why I am in prison

COLOSSIANS 4:3 NCV

He said to them, "Go into all the world. Preach the good news to everyone."

MARK 16:15 NIrV

So many people have no idea what it means to have the Spirit of Christ in their hearts. It is our job, as the voice and hands of God, to let people know the truth of Christ, so they, too, might come to put their trust in Him.

Help me to teach others by the example of my life what it means to be a Christian. I will put my trust in You. Help me to share that trust with others. Amen.

. . . .

. . . .

. . . .

. . . .

. . . .

. . . .

. . . .

. . . .

. . . .

. . . .

. . . .

. . . .

Day 58
LOVING OTHERS

....

Jesus replied: " 'Love the Lord your God with all your heart and with all your soul and with all your mind.' This is the first and greatest commandment. And the second is like it: 'Love your neighbor as yourself.' "

MATTHEW 22:37–39 NIV

Dear children, let's not merely say that we love each other; let us show the truth by our actions.

1 JOHN 3:18 NLT

People say love is a decision. Sounds simple enough, right? The fact is that telling others we love them and showing that love are two very different realities. Jesus is the embodiment of active love. He loved those who were thought most unlovable. And we are called to do the same.

Lord, let me be intentional, active, and willing to put aside my own desires so that I can love others better. Amen.

....
....
....
....
....
....
....
....
....

GOD'S CORRECTION

* *

For whom the LORD loveth he correcteth; even as a father the son in whom he delighteth.

PROVERBS 3:12 KJV

Thou shalt also consider in thine heart, that, as a man chasteneth his son,
so the LORD thy God chasteneth thee. Therefore thou shalt keep the
commandments of the LORD thy God, to walk in his ways, and to fear him.

DEUTERONOMY 8:5–6 KJV

Often God tries to gently lead us along the path of goodness, but we resist. Many times the only way to get our attention is through a stinging blow. It is never out of anger, but always out of love.

*B*reak my spirit of defiance, no matter what it takes, so that I might openly receive every instruction that You give. Amen.

Day 60
BELIEF

And Jesus said to him, " 'If you can'! All things are possible for one who believes."

MARK 9:23 ESV

For we did not follow cleverly devised stories when we told you about the coming of our Lord Jesus Christ in power, but we were eyewitnesses of his majesty.

2 PETER 1:16 NIV

It's not uncommon to run into people who claim the Bible is a collection of fairy tales. But remember, you, like the apostles, are an eyewitness. You were there when Jesus saved you. And you have testimonies from those who observed Jesus' ministry. When people wonder why you believe, tell them.

When others act as if I'm crazy to believe in You, help me not to be offended, Lord. Instead, help me to show them Your truth. Amen.

....
....
....
....
....
....
....
....
....
....
....

*Don't get tired of helping others. You will be rewarded when
the time is right, if you don't give up.*

GALATIANS 6:9 CEV

*"I tell you, use the riches of this world to help others. In that way, you will make
friends for yourselves. Then when your riches are gone, you will be
welcomed into your eternal home in heaven."*

LUKE 16:9 NIrV

We are given so many opportunities to help others. Jesus said that every time we help
any person in need, it is as if we have done it for Christ Himself. Let us always reach
out and take hold of the chances we have for serving others.

*L ord, so often I turn from those in need. Open my eyes and my heart that I might extend
the hand of Christ to them. Amen.*

Day 62
GUIDANCE

And thine ears shall hear a word behind thee, saying, This is the way,
walk ye in it, when ye turn to the right hand, and when ye turn to the left.

Isaiah 30.21 kjv

A man's heart deviseth his way: but the Lord directeth his steps.

Proverbs 16:9 kjv

In our lives, we need to learn to let the Lord rule. Giving God control is not a sign of weakness; it is the greatest show of strength we will ever make. Under the guidance of God, we become conquerors in a world that tries hard to break us down.

Heavenly Father, do not let me be swayed from the path You have set me on. Others may fail me, but You never will. Hallelujah! Amen.

*But if anyone has the world's goods and sees his brother in need,
yet closes his heart against him, how does God's love abide in him?*

1 JOHN 3:17 ESV

*The more you have, the more people come to help you spend it.
So what good is wealth—except perhaps to watch it slip through your fingers!*

ECCLESIASTES 5:11 NLT

Making money doesn't result in financial stability. Wealth runs through our fingers as we spend more than we make and wonder how we will pay for everything. It's time for us to put the principles we know into action. God gives us joy in our possessions. He only asks us to use them wisely.

Jehovah Jireh, the Lord who provides, we thank You for Your provision. Teach us to value the eternal over the temporal. Amen.

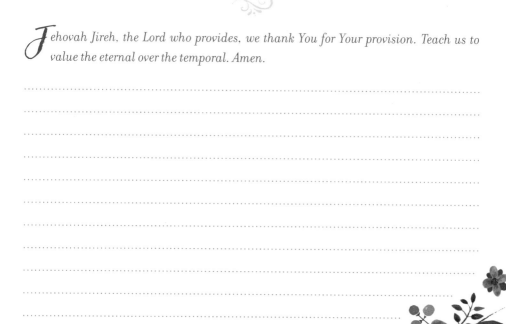

Day 64
PRAYER

I am the one who has seen the afflictions that come from the rod of the LORD's anger. . . .
He has walled me in, and I cannot escape. He has bound me in heavy chains.
And though I cry and shout, he has shut out my prayers. . . . Yet I still dare
to hope when I remember this: The faithful love of the LORD never ends!

LAMENTATIONS 3:1, 7–8, 21–22 NLT

I will answer their prayers before they finish praying.

ISAIAH 65:24 CEV

God alone knows what we need before we ask. He even knows what we need before we know the need. Life may take us by surprise, but never the Lord God who knows the end from the beginning. He knows what's behind, what's ahead, and what's now—and He will hear your prayers.

I praise You, Lord, that You surround me through all of life. Keep my eyes of faith on You, I pray. Amen.

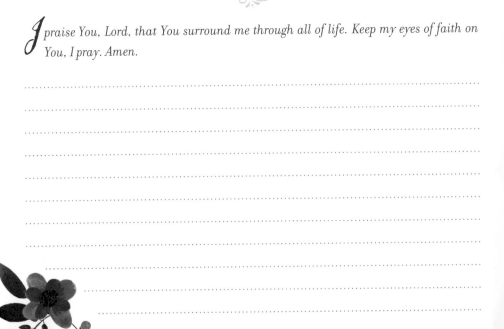

When Pharaoh let the people go, God did not lead them on the road through the Philistine country, though that was shorter. For God said, "If they face war, they might change their minds and return to Egypt."

EXODUS 13:17 NIV

To everything there is a season, a time for every purpose under heaven.

ECCLESIASTES 3:1 NKJV

Change is a regular part of modern life. Jobs shift or disappear. Friends move. Babies are born, and children graduate and marry. Only one thing in our lives never changes: God. When our world swirls and threatens to shift out of control, we can know that God is never surprised, never caught off guard by anything that happens.

Lord, help me remember Your love and guidance when my life turns upside down. Grant me wisdom for the journey and a hope for the future. Amen.

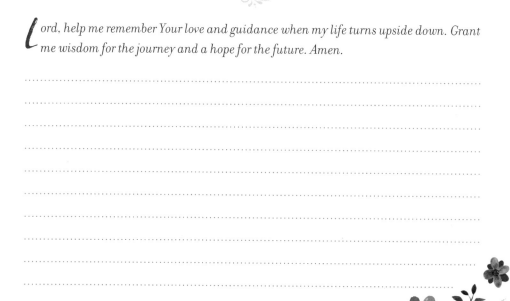

Day 66
GOD'S PRESENCE

....

But now God has made you his friends again. He did this through Christ's death
in the body so that he might bring you into God's presence as people who are holy,
with no wrong, and with nothing of which God can judge you guilty.

COLOSSIANS 1:22 NCV

Then the LORD God Almighty will be with you, just as you say he is.

AMOS 5:14 NIV

Sometimes we have trouble feeling God's presence, especially in troublesome situations.
God has told us that He will never leave us. So if we feel as if God is not near, perhaps
the distance is of our own choosing. Look into the goodness of God's Word. Seek His
face. Proclaim that He is standing by your side. And He will be, just as you have said.

Thank You, Lord, for always being with me. With You by my side, I will live! I will
overcome all. Thank You for being immovable. Amen.

....
....
....
....
....
....
....
....
....
....

Solomon rode high on a crest of popular acclaim—it was all GOD's doing.
GOD gave him position and honor beyond any king in Israel before him.

1 CHRONICLES 29:25 MSG

"Your Father, who sees what is done in secret, will reward you."

MATTHEW 6:6 NIV

Perhaps your behind-the-scenes sacrifices are going unnoticed by the world. Do not give up and think it doesn't matter. It matters to God. Seek to please Him above anyone else, and your life will honor Him.

L ord, may what I do in secret bring glory to You. May I not seek man's approval, but Yours alone. Amen.

Day 68
FRIENDSHIP

"And I tell you, make friends for yourselves by means of unrighteous wealth, so that when it fails they may receive you into the eternal dwellings."

LUKE 16:9 ESV

Three of Job's friends heard of all the trouble that had fallen on him. Each traveled from his own country. . .and went together to Job to keep him company and comfort him.

JOB 2:11 MSG

We can become so wrapped up in the tasks we are trying to achieve that we forget that life is about people—the relationships—God has put around us. We need each other—as friends, family, or just passing acquaintances—in order to live successful lives. God measures His wealth in souls. That should be our focus, too.

Lord, help me to know when it's time to drop the task and run to the relationship. Amen.

"For the vision is yet for the appointed time; it hastens toward the goal and it will not fail. Though it tarries, wait for it; for it will certainly come, it will not delay."

HABAKKUK 2:3 NASB

What joy for those whose strength comes from the LORD, who have set their minds on a pilgrimage to Jerusalem. When they walk through the Valley of Weeping, it will become a place of refreshing springs. The autumn rains will clothe it with blessings.

PSALM 84:5–6 NLT

Have you ever questioned God when your goals and plans were altered? We all have disappointments and failures, but God never fails us. Our disappointment will form pools of blessings when we continue on God's path despite dashed dreams.

Heavenly Father, help me to surrender my dreams and goals to You. When my dreams evaporate, please turn my weeping into blessings. Amen.

Day 70
COMPASSION

Light shines in the darkness for the godly.
They are generous, compassionate, and righteous.

PSALM 112:4 NLT

Is there any encouragement from belonging to Christ? Any comfort from his love?
Any fellowship together in the Spirit? Are your hearts tender and compassionate?
Then make me truly happy by agreeing wholeheartedly with each other,
loving one another, and working together with one mind and purpose.

PHILIPPIANS 2:1–2 NLT

People who suffer greatly need our compassion and love, but instead they often receive our judgment and condemnation. Christ does not ask us to accept sin or the results of sin, but He commands us to love the one who sins.

Lord, let compassion rule in my heart as I face a sinful world. I am a sinner, too, and only through Your infinite love am I made whole. Amen.

God Most High, I will rejoice; I will celebrate and sing because of you.

Psalm 9:2 cev

The LORD has done it this very day; let us rejoice today and be glad.

Psalm 118:24 niv

God made a glorious today for us. Now it's our responsibility to rejoice in it. What's holding you back from finding gladness in the dawn of each new morning?

Father, help me always to put my problems in perspective with a giant dose of rejoicing in You. Amen.

Day 72
COMPARISON

. . . .

If we live in the Spirit, let us also walk in the Spirit. Let us not be desirous of vain glory, provoking one another, envying one another.

GALATIANS 5:25–26 KJV

It is obvious what kind of life develops out of trying to get your own way all the time. . . cutthroat competition. . .the vicious habit of depersonalizing everyone into a rival. . . . If you use your freedom this way, you will not inherit God's kingdom.

GALATIANS 5:19–21 MSG

It is important to run your own race, at your own pace—not too fast, but not too slowly, either. Try not to compare yourself too closely with others. We are all at different stages on our own courses. You can learn from those who have gone before, and you have the privilege of teaching those who come behind.

Lord, give me the strength I need to finish my race and the wisdom I need to run it well. And help me to be an encouragement to others. Amen.

. . . .
. . . .
. . . .
. . . .
. . . .
. . . .
. . . .
. . . .
. . . .

*God's plan was to make me a servant of his church and to send me
to preach his complete message to you.*

COLOSSIANS 1:25 CEV

*[God] has made everything beautiful in its time. He has also set eternity in the
human heart; yet no one can fathom what God has done from beginning to end.*

ECCLESIASTES 3:11 NIV

The more exhausted we are, the harder it is to remember that God has a plan for us
and that we are living that plan every day. We are unable to see "the big picture" of
our lives, what God has in store for us, and how what we do every day fits into His
plan. We have to trust in His wisdom and keep on the journey He has set before us.

*ord, guide my steps so that everything I do reveals my love for You and my faith in Your
plan for my life. Amen.*

. . . .

. . . .

. . . .

. . . .

. . . .

. . . .

. . . .

. . . .

. . . .

. . . .

Day 74
GOD'S WORD

"Have faith in me, and you will have life-giving water flowing from deep inside you, just as the Scriptures say."

JOHN 7:38 CEV

Above all, you must realize that no prophecy in Scripture ever came from the prophet's own understanding, or from human initiative. No, those prophets were moved by the Holy Spirit, and they spoke from God.

2 PETER 1:20–21 NLT

God gave us the Bible to serve us much as an anchor serves a boat. The Bible is filled with valuable information for your mission on earth. God's Word can set your mind at peace and hold you steady through life's storms. It is assurance that no matter what you face in this battle of life, God will bring you safely home.

God, I know the Bible is true and full of wisdom for my life. Help me to grow and understand what I read and apply it to my life. Amen.

. . . .

. . . .

. . . .

. . . .

. . . .

. . . .

. . . .

. . . .

. . . .

My son, attend to my words; incline thine ear unto my sayings. . . . For they are life unto those that find them, and health to all their flesh. Keep thy heart with all diligence; for out of it are the issues of life.

PROVERBS 4:20, 22–23 KJV

Don't you realize that your body is the temple of the Holy Spirit. . . .You do not belong to yourself, for God bought you with a high price. So you must honor God with your body.

1 CORINTHIANS 6:19–20 NLT

God, in His infinite wisdom, created us with certain bodily needs to teach us discipline. We need to institute physical disciplines like exercise, diet, and rest to properly care for the temple of the Holy Spirit—our bodies. While those actions will attend to the needs of the body, prayer, fasting, and fellowship will attend to the spirit.

Father, forgive me for not caring for Your temple as I should. Help me to make time in my life for those simple disciplines. Amen.

Day 76
PRIDE

···

"Those who exalt themselves will be humbled,
and those who humble themselves will be exalted."

MATTHEW 23:12 NIV

Then [Jesus] said to them, "Whoever welcomes this little child in my name
welcomes me; and whoever welcomes me welcomes the one who sent me.
For it is the one who is least among you all who is the greatest."

LUKE 9:48 NIV

Often people view themselves and their daily activities as more important than someone else's. Jesus' mentality was the exact opposite. He promised that the last would be first. Glorify Him today by humbling yourself.

Lord, give me humility as I interact with people today. Amen.

···
···
···
···
···
···
···
···
···
···
···
···

That I may publish with the voice of thanksgiving,
and tell of all thy wondrous works.

PSALM 26:7 KJV

Daniel answered and said: "Blessed be the name of God forever
and ever, for wisdom and might are His."

DANIEL 2:20 NKJV

Though God is great, He doesn't appreciate being taken for granted any more than we would. When God brings us through a trial, do we worship Him with great thankfulness, or do we take that blessing as our due? And when He responds to ordinary situations, do we give thanks?

Make me thankful, Lord, for all the ways in which You bless and care for me. I don't want my life to become laden with ungratefulness. Amen.

Day 78
TRIALS

So that no one would be unsettled by these trials.
For you know quite well that we are destined for them.

1 Thessalonians 3:3 niv

God will bless you, if you don't give up when your faith is being tested.
He will reward you with a glorious life, just as he rewards everyone who loves him.

James 1:12 cev

God never tests us beyond our level of endurance. He is faithful to see us through each hardship and to bless us richly when our trial is through. The nighttimes of our life may seem dismal and black, but there is always a glorious morning on the rise.

*W*hen times seem exceptionally difficult, Lord, help me to remember that they will pass away. No trial lasts forever, Lord, and the promise of good things to come is mine. Amen.

"You must not worship any of the gods of neighboring nations, for the LORD your God, who lives among you, is a jealous God. His anger will flare up against you, and he will wipe you from the face of the earth."

DEUTERONOMY 6:14–15 NLT

We wither beneath your anger; we are overwhelmed by your fury. You spread out our sins before you—our secret sins—and you see them all. We live our lives beneath your wrath, ending our years with a groan.

PSALM 90:7–9 NLT

God tells us it is okay to be angry, but we are not to sin. We need to have a spirit of reconciliation, making amends and compromising. When we don't have this perspective of quickly resolving conflict, our anger festers. We end up making room for the devil, allowing Satan to have a foothold in our lives.

Forgiving Lord, I surrender my anger to You. Please give me a spirit of reconciliation and the opportunity to make amends. Amen.

....

....

....

....

....

....

....

....

....

Day 80
SPIRITUAL REFRESHMENT

Therefore we have been comforted in your comfort. And we rejoiced exceedingly more for the joy of Titus, because his spirit has been refreshed by you all.

2 Corinthians 7:13 nkjv

Do not be wise in your own eyes; fear the Lord and shun evil. This will bring health to your body and nourishment to your bones.

Proverbs 3:7–8 niv

Just as we exercise to strengthen our bodies, we must use our spiritual muscles to attain the strength and peace we all need and desire. As we pray, read, and meditate on God's Word, we increase our spiritual stamina. Although our circumstances may not change, the Lord gives us a new perspective filled with hope.

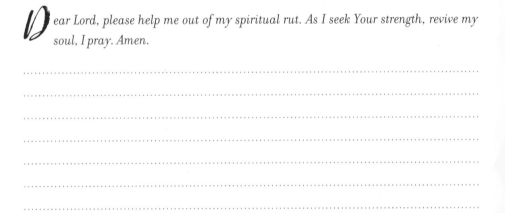

Dear Lord, please help me out of my spiritual rut. As I seek Your strength, revive my soul, I pray. Amen.

"Remember, Lord, how I have walked before you faithfully and with wholehearted devotion and have done what is good in your eyes." And Hezekiah wept bitterly.

2 Kings 20:3 niv

Let us hold unswervingly to the hope we profess, for he who promised is faithful.

Hebrews 10:23 niv

Sometimes just a whisper from Satan, the father of lies, can cause shakiness where once there was steadfastness. Place your hope in Christ alone. He will help you to resist the lies of this world. Hold unswervingly to your Savior today. He is faithful!

Jesus, You are the object of my hope. There are many distractions in my life, but I pray that You will help me to keep my eyes on You. Amen.

Day 82
TEMPTATION

Don't blame God when you are tempted! God cannot be tempted by evil, and he doesn't use evil to tempt others. We are tempted by our own desires that drag us off and trap us. Our desires make us sin, and when sin is finished with us, it leaves us dead.

JAMES 1:13–15 CEV

Because he himself suffered when he was tempted, he is able to help those who are being tempted.

HEBREWS 2:18 NIV

God gives us the reason to say no. So many people would lead us from the path of God. Ask the Lord for guidance. In the face of our strongest temptations, God will give us strength and the reason to resist.

O God, help me to free myself from those things I know displease You. Guide me, strengthen me, liberate me, I pray. Amen.

....

....

....

....

....

....

....

....

....

....

"The Lord is my strength and song, and He has become my salvation."

Exodus 15:2 nkjv

The Spirit and the bride say, "Come!" And let the one who hears say, "Come!"
Let the one who is thirsty come; and let the one who wishes
take the free gift of the water of life.

Revelation 22:17 niv

As we drink deeply of the water of life, we recognize God's great gift. Grateful, we seek out ways to serve Him. But even if we gave all we had, we could never repay God. His gift of salvation would still be free.

Thank You, Lord, for giving me the free gift of salvation—the best gift anyone could offer. Amen.

Day 84
GENEROSITY

It is well with the man who deals generously and lends. . . .He has distributed freely; he has given to the poor; his righteousness endures forever; his horn is exalted in honor.

PSALM 112:5, 9 ESV

Honor the LORD from your wealth and from the first of all your produce; so your barns will be filled with plenty and your vats will overflow with new wine.

PROVERBS 3:9–10 NASB

The truth is that everything we have comes from God. The Bible calls us to cheerfully give back to the Lord one-tenth of all we earn. Giving to God has great reward. When believers honor God by giving to Him, we can trust that He will provide for our needs.

Lord, remind me not to separate my finances from my faith. All that I have comes from Your hand, and I should give generously from what You have entrusted to me. Amen.

*"Be sure you do not do good things in front of others just to be seen by them.
If you do, you have no reward from your Father in heaven."*

Matthew 6:1 nlv

Knowledge makes us proud of ourselves, while love makes us helpful to others.

1 Corinthians 8:1 cev

We all need help. We can't do life alone. And perhaps that is a great blessing to realize. God never meant for us to do it alone! He designed us to live in community—family, friends, and church—helping and serving and meeting one another's needs.

Lord, You promise never to leave us nor forsake us. Thank You for providing helpers to come alongside of me. Amen.

Day 86
FAITH

*For verily I say unto you, That whosoever shall say unto this mountain,
Be thou removed, and be thou cast intothe sea; and shall not doubt
in his heart, but shall believe that those things which he saith
shall come to pass;he shall have whatsoever he saith.*

MARK 11:23 KJV

*[Jesus] replied, "If you have faith as small as a mustard seed,
you can say to this mulberry tree, 'Be uprooted and
planted in the sea,' and it will obey you."*

LUKE 17:6 NIV

The Lord understands the limitations of our humanity. Surely it was not happenstance that Christ chose a seed as His example when teaching about faith. A mustard seed is one of the tiniest of all seeds, yet even mustard seed-sized faith can accomplish great things.

Father, I cannot see You with my eyes, but I know You are there. Increase my faith, I pray. Amen.

....

....

....

....

....

....

....

....

*"Come to Me, all you who labor and are heavy laden, and I will give you rest.
Take My yoke upon you and learn from Me, for I am gentle and
lowly in heart, and you will find rest for your souls."*

MATTHEW 11:28–29 NKJV

*I know that nothing is better for them than to rejoice, and to do good in their lives,
and also that every man should eat and drink and enjoy
the good of all his labor—it is the gift of God.*

ECCLESIASTES 3:12–13 NKJV

Constant work is not what God intended for our lives. We should work hard, yes, but not to the exclusion of rest and times of renewal for our minds and souls. Our food, homes, and friendships are gifts that God meant for us to enjoy. Finding time isn't always easy, but the rewards of a calmer mind and a grateful heart will be well worth the effort.

ord, thank You for the gifts You've bestowed on me. Help me find moments to enjoy them. Amen.

Day 88
FEAR

*Yea, though I walk through the valley of the shadow of death, I will fear no evil:
for thou art with me; thy rod and thy staff they comfort me.*

PSALM 23:4 KJV

*The LORD is my light and my salvation; whom shall I fear? The LORD is the defense of my life;
whom shall I dread? When evildoers came upon me to devour my flesh, my adversaries
and my enemies, they stumbled and fell. Though a host encamp against me, my heart will
not fear; though war arise against me, in spite of this I shall be confident.*

PSALM 27:1–3 NASB

Fear is a paralyzing thing. The specific thing that frightens us is as individual and
unique as people, but we all struggle with fear at some time in our lives. As Christians,
we can take the admonition "Fear not" to heart. God knows our fears and encourages
us to turn fear into faith.

Thank You, Lord, for Your faithfulness and love that casts out fear. Amen.

. . . .
. . . .
. . . .
. . . .
. . . .
. . . .
. . . .
. . . .
. . . .

*"Therefore I tell you, do not worry about your life, what you will eat or drink;
or about your body, what you will wear. Is not life more
than food, and the body more than clothes?"*

MATTHEW 6:25 NIV

But stop worrying! Just remember what the LORD your God did to Egypt and its king.

DEUTERONOMY 7:18 CEV

No matter how bleak the world looks, no matter what crisis we are going through, we do not have to worry, for although heaven and earth may pass away, God's words—the anchor of our spirit, the bread of our lives, that which gives us peace beyond understanding—will remain forever.

Lord, thank You for being my rock, my refuge, and my rest. Amen.

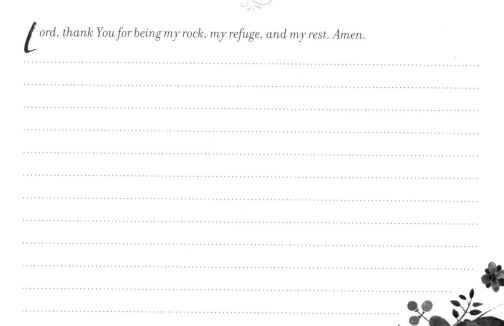

Day 90
PRIORITIES

If you make Insight your priority, and won't take no for an answer,
searching for it like a prospector panning for gold, like an adventurer
on a treasure hunt, believe me, before you know it Fear-of-God will
be yours; you'll have come upon the Knowledge of God.

PROVERBS 2:3–5 MSG

"But seek first the kingdom of God and his righteousness,
and all these things will be added to you."

MATTHEW 6:33 ESV

Jesus asks for the unexpected. He may ask us for our things, our time, or our talents. He asks us to align our use of what He has given us with His priorities. We can't predict when or how Jesus will call on us to serve Him. What does the Master need? That should become our priority.

*M*aster of all, we invite You to be the Master of our hearts, of everything we possess and are. Teach us to make Your priorities our own. Amen.

*"Honor your father and your mother, that your days may be long
in the land that the LORD your God is giving you."*

EXODUS 20:12 ESV

Gray hair is a crown of splendor; it is attained in the way of righteousness.

PROVERBS 16:31 NIV

As we age physically, our spiritual growth should correspond. The seed of faith planted in our hearts is meant to germinate, bud, and bloom over the natural course of time. And gray hair—the evidence that God has been cultivating us both physically and spiritually—is the crowning touch.

Father, as I age, teach me to wear spiritual maturity as a crown. Physically, help me learn to rejoice in what is remaining rather than lament what is lost. Amen.

Day 92
DEATH

···

Yea, though I walk through the valley of the shadow of death, I will fear no evil:
for thou art with me; thy rod and thy staff they comfort me.

PSALM 23:4 KJV

The life of mortals is like grass, they flourish like a flower of the field;
the wind blows over it and it is gone, and its place remembers it no more.

PSALM 103:15–16 NIV

Our lives begin and end in the blink of an eye. The things that we think are so important may one day be merely trivial. All that will matter is that we told others about Christ. Our mission is to do the will of God, to go where God is working, and to make a difference for Him.

Lord, I am willing to make an eternal difference for You. Amen.

*For this very reason, make every effort to add to your faith goodness;
and to goodness, knowledge; and to knowledge, self-control; and to self-control,
perseverance; and to perseverance, godliness; and to godliness,
mutual affection; and to mutual affection, love.*

2 PETER 1:5–7 NIV

*But if anyone has the world's goods and sees his brother in need,
yet closes his heart against him, how does God's love abide in him?*

1 JOHN 3:17 ESV

Because of God's love, Jesus paid an overwhelming debt He didn't owe through His death on the cross. The apostle Paul admonishes us to incur a debt we can never pay—the debt of continuing love. Love is the only debt God encourages. In this instance, we can never owe enough.

Dear Lord, thank You for the price You paid for me. May I increase the debt of love I owe to others. Amen.

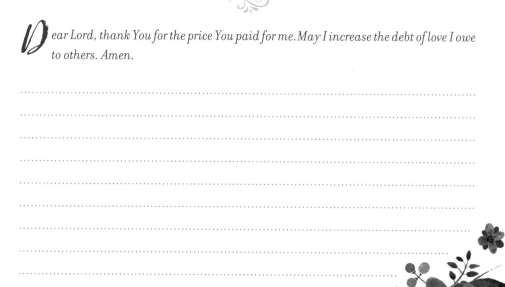

Day 94
PEACE

*These things I have spoken unto you, that in me ye might have peace. In the world
ye shall have tribulation: but be of good cheer; I have overcome the world.*

JOHN 16:33 KJV

Those who love Your law have great peace, and nothing causes them to stumble.

PSALM 119:165 NASB

God's desire is not to overwhelm you. He recommends that you do your very best to
lead a quiet, simple life while you work hard at the things you need to do. Find peace
as you release yourself from self-imposed requirements and surrender to God's will.

*Heavenly Father, please help me to order my life in such a way that I bring peace to my
life and to the lives of those around me. Amen.*

Then the Lord God said, "It is not good for the man to be alone;
I will make him a helper suitable for him."

GENESIS 2:18 NASB

God makes a home for the lonely.

PSALM 68:6 AMP

The Lord made people to have relationships with Himself and others, and He recognizes and provides for our need for human companionship. His best prescription for loneliness: relationships with Him and with His people.

Father, sometimes I struggle with feeling alone. In those times, help me to reach out to Your love and to the companionship of fellow believers. Amen.

Day 96
FRIENDSHIP

"When I was in my prime, God's friendship was felt in my home."

JOB 29:4 NLT

*"I no longer call you slaves, because a master doesn't confide in his slaves.
Now you are my friends, since I have told you everything the Father told me."*

JOHN 15:15 NLT

One of the first casualties of a busy life is friendship. Often we don't even realize it is missing, because the more activities we have, the more people who surround us. We all have a need for close friendships. We need others in our lives who will challenge us to make us sharper, bolder, gentler, and more Christlike.

D ear Jesus, I know You are a friend who sticks closer than a brother, yet sometimes I need the comfort of friends I can see and touch. Help me to invest in friends. Amen.

Epaphras, who is one of you and a servant of Christ Jesus, sends greetings.
He is always wrestling in prayer for you, that you may stand
firm in all the will of God, mature and fully assured.

COLOSSIANS 4:12 NIV

"I looked for someone among them who would build up the wall and stand before me
in the gap on behalf of the land so I would not have to destroy it, but I found no one."

EZEKIEL 22:30 NIV

It's easy in the busyness of life to overlook a prayer request someone else has made. Take time right when you receive a request to talk to the Lord on the requester's behalf. Be the bridge that carries that person through the valley of darkness back to the mountaintop of joy.

Heavenly Father, help me to have a heart of compassion. Help me never to be too busy to pray for those I know and even those I don't know who need Your comfort. Amen.

Day 98
FALSE TEACHING

But there were also false prophets in Israel, just as there will be false teachers among you. They will cleverly teach destructive heresies and even deny the Master who bought them. . . . Many will follow their evil teaching and shameful immorality. And because of these teachers, the way of truth will be slandered.

2 Peter 2:1–2 nlt

Dear friends, do not believe every spirit, but test the spirits to see whether they are from God . . . . This is how you can recognize the Spirit of God: Every spirit that acknowledges that Jesus Christ has come in the flesh is from God.

1 John 4:1–2 niv

We know false teaching is out there, but how can we identify it and avoid wrong theology? When we know God's Word well, false teaching will jump out at us. Anything that does not agree with scripture is in the wrong.

*F*ather, my desire is to learn Your Word well so that I remain faithful to Your teaching. Amen.

....
....
....
....
....
....
....
....
....
....

If a man does not repent, God will whet his sword; he has bent and readied his bow.

Psalm 7:12 esv

Return to the Lord your God, for he is merciful and compassionate, slow to get angry and filled with unfailing love. He is eager to relent and not punish.

Joel 2:13 nlt

When God commands us to repent, He doesn't want a mumbled apology. He doesn't even want demonstrative tears—unless they come from a repentant heart. Repentance from sinning against God involves a willful action, a changing of direction.

Forgive me, Lord. Help me turn from my sin. Amen.

. . . .
. . . .
. . . .
. . . .
. . . .
. . . .
. . . .
. . . .
. . . .
. . . .
. . . .
. . . .
. . . .

Day 100
MIRACLES

Our Lord, no other gods compare with you—Majestic and holy!
Fearsome and glorious! Miracle worker!

Exodus 15:11 cev

"God does wonders that cannot be understood;
he does so many miracles they cannot be counted."

Job 5:9 ncv

The word *miracle* sounds strange in this day and age. If only people would open their hearts and begin looking more deeply than they are able with their eyes alone. A beautiful sunset, the wonder of human life: these are miracles in a sense, and they are evidence of the wonder of God.

Make me a believer, Lord. Show me the multitude of miracles You have created and are creating. Amen.

RESPONSIBILITY

*Make a careful exploration of who you are and the work you have been given,
and then sink yourself into that. Don't be impressed with yourself.
Don't compare yourself with others. Each of you must take responsibility
for doing the creative best you can with your own life.*

Galatians 6:4–5 msg

*Because of the transgression of a land, many are its princes;
but by a man of understanding and knowledge right will be prolonged.*

Proverbs 28:2 nkjv

God raises up individuals in families, at work, at church, and in government to
become leaders. Whatever our jobs are, we are responsible. How we behave and what
we believe not only influence us but those we come into contact with.

Lord, give me seeing eyes and hearing ears to guide others. Amen.

Day 102
ADDICTION

Do not join those who drink too much wine or gorge themselves on meat,
for drunkards and gluttons become poor, and drowsiness clothes them in rags.

PROVERBS 23:20–21 NIV

Let us behave decently, as in the daytime, not in carousing and drunkenness,
not in sexual immorality and debauchery, not in dissension and jealousy.

ROMANS 13:13 NIV

Struggling with addiction is tough. Don't do it alone. Having someone to hold you accountable could be the extra support necessary to remain steadfast.

Father, I wish to be free from addiction. Help me to seek out trusted friends and counselors to hold my hand and keep me accountable. Amen.

*When thou liest down, thou shalt not be afraid: yea, thou shalt lie down,
and thy sleep shall be sweet.*

PROVERBS 3:24 KJV

*For he spake in a certain place of the seventh day on this wise, and God did rest the
seventh day from all his works. . . . There remaineth therefore a rest to the people of God.*

HEBREWS 4:4, 9 KJV

It takes more than a quiet place or a time away to bring true rest. We must jump into
God's everlasting arms and dive into His Word. Rest is found in knowing Christ and
understanding that through His sacrifice we are at peace. As we allow God's peace
to fill us, we will find real rest.

*Father God, there are many days when I don't have time to sit. In all these times,
remind me that peace comes from knowing You and resting in the work You have
done. Amen.*

Day 104
FINANCES

"Do not worry then, saying, 'What will we eat?' or 'What will we drink?' or
'What will we wear for clothing?'. . .for your heavenly Father knows that
you need all those things. But seek first His kingdom and
His righteousness, and all these things will be added to you."

MATTHEW 6:31–33 NASB

I consider everything a loss because of the surpassing worth of knowing Christ Jesus
my Lord, for whose sake I have lost all things. I consider them
garbage, that I may gain Christ.

PHILIPPIANS 3:8 NIV

Are you a good steward of your finances? Ask the Lord to help you control your spending by leading you into wise decisions. He wants you to enjoy the beautiful things He created, but only after you have learned that they mean nothing compared to the treasure found in Christ.

Father, thank You for all Your blessings. Help me to spend wisely and to remain focused on the greatest treasure—You. Amen.

For He made Him who knew no sin to be sin for us,
that we might become the righteousness of God in Him.

2 Corinthians 5:21 nkjv

For a man's ways are before the eyes of the Lord, and he ponders all his paths.
The iniquities of the wicked ensnare him, and he is held fast in the cords of his sin.

Proverbs 5:21–22 esv

It is not enough to try not to sin, but we should do everything in our power to avoid it, turn from it, move as far away from it as possible, and leave it as far behind as we can. It is by a conscious effort that we avoid sin, just as it is by choice that we do good.

May I choose the right path, almighty God, turning from what I know You would not have me do. Amen.

. . . .
. . . .
. . . .
. . . .
. . . .
. . . .
. . . .
. . . .
. . . .
. . . .
. . . .
. . . .

Day 106
ABIDING

....

*"I have come as a light into the world,
that whoever believes in Me should not abide in darkness."*

JOHN 12:46 NKJV

*"If you abide in Me, and My words abide in you,
you will ask what you desire, and it shall be done for you."*

JOHN 15:7 NKJV

Abiding is an active practice of trust in God that demands much of us but also provides us with untold blessings.

Heavenly Father, strengthen me to abide in You. I cannot do it on my own, but only with Your support. Amen.

....
....
....
....
....
....
....
....
....
....
....
....
....

* * *

*For we are God's masterpiece. He has created us anew in Christ Jesus,
so we can do the good things he planned for us long ago.*

EPHESIANS 2:10 NLT

*"I know what I'm doing. I have it all planned out—plans to take care of you,
not abandon you, plans to give you the future you hope for."*

JEREMIAH 29:10–11 MSG

We humans have such limited vision. God sees the big picture. Be open. Be flexible. Allow God to change your plans in order to accomplish His divine purposes. Instead of becoming frustrated, look for ways the Lord might be working.

Dear Lord, forgive me when I become so rigidly locked in my own agenda that I miss Yours. Give me Your eternal perspective so that I may be open to divine interruptions. Amen.

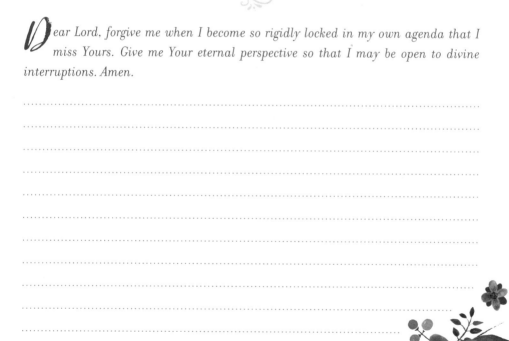

Day 108
FAMILY

Then the LORD God made a woman from the rib he had taken out of the man,
and he brought her to the man. The man said, "This is now bone of my bones
and flesh of my flesh; she shall be called 'woman,' for she was taken out of
man." That is why a man leaves his father and mother and is
united to his wife, and they become one flesh.

GENESIS 2:22–24 NIV

I will instruct you and teach you in the way you should go;
I will counsel you with my loving eye on you.

PSALM 32:8 NIV

Even good things, like enjoying your work, can crowd out the best things, like loving your family. When God rings a warning bell that we are neglecting areas of importance, we need to listen gratefully and hasten to make changes before it's too late.

Fix my attention, Lord! Help me to identify my imbalances and areas of neglect. Amen.

· ·

*If my people, which are called by my name, shall humble themselves, and pray,
and seek my face, and turn from their wicked ways; then will I hear
from heaven, and will forgive their sin, and will heal their land.*

2 Chronicles 7:14 kjv

*"He who is not with Me is against Me; and he who does not gather with Me scatters.
Therefore I say to you, any sin and blasphemy shall be forgiven people, but blasphemy
against the Spirit shall not be forgiven."*

Matthew 12:30–31 nasb

If we are not humbled by the greatness of God's forgiveness, we need to question
whether we have a relationship with Him or not.

L ord, thank You for forgiveness. I am unworthy, yet You love me. Amen.

· ·

· ·

· ·

· ·

· ·

· ·

· ·

· ·

· ·

· ·

· ·

Day 110
GOD'S PRESENCE

"The Lord your God goes with you; he will never leave you nor forsake you."

DEUTERONOMY 31:6 NIV

*My dear friends, if our hearts do not make us feel guilty,
we can come without fear into God's presence.*

1 JOHN 3:21 NCV

While we're doing life on our own, we can forget that God is standing there waiting to do life every day with us. If you feel distant from God today, look up. He's waiting for you to find your rightful place with Him.

God, I never want to become so busy that I lose sight of You. Amen.

*After he was raised from the dead, his disciples recalled what he had said.
Then they believed the scripture and the words that Jesus had spoken.*

JOHN 2:22 NIV

*Then Jesus spoke to them again, saying, "I am the light of the world. He who follows
Me shall not walk in darkness, but have the light of life."*

JOHN 8:12 NKJV

We can be thankful for the light that illuminates our path—the Word of God. Without
it we would stumble along through life not knowing which paths to take in a world
that sometimes looks dark and scary.

*Heavenly Father, thank You for Your Word that is a lamp unto my feet and a light unto
my path. Amen.*

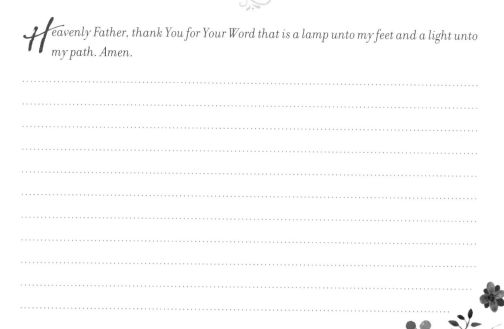

Day 112
SPIRITUAL FRUIT

Blessed is the one who does not walk in step with the wicked. . .but whose delight
is in the law of the Lord, and who meditates on his law day and night.

PSALM 1:1–2 NIV

You did not choose me. I chose you and sent you out to produce fruit, the kind of fruit
that will last. Then my Father will give you whatever you ask for in my name.

JOHN 15:16 CEV

Whether or not we expect to be, we are spiritual fruit producers. As we live day by day, others can see the love, faith, and goodness that flow from our lives as we serve Jesus. As we grow in Him, our lives testify to His greatness and the work He's doing in our lives.

Father, help me to cultivate spiritual fruit in my life so that I declare Your greatness to those I meet. Amen.

. . . .

And I will bring the blind by a way that they knew not; I will lead them in paths that they have not known: I will make darkness light before them, and crooked things straight. These things will I do unto them, and not forsake them.

Isaiah 42:16 KJV

When Jesus spoke again to the people, he said, "I am the light of the world. Whoever follows me will never walk in darkness, but will have the light of life."

John 8:12 NIV

Jesus said followers will never have to walk in darkness again but will have a life in the light. No more stumbling—we have His guidance. His light of life is a vibrant life lived confidently because we can see the path before us through eyes of faith.

Light of life, thank You that we do not hover in darkness any longer. In You we walk boldly in the light of life, forgiven, free, and vibrant. Amen.

....
....
....
....
....
....
....
....
....
....
....

Day 114
COMFORT

Even though I walk through the darkest valley, I will fear no evil,
for you are with me; your rod and your staff, they comfort me.

PSALM 23:4 NIV

You have allowed me to suffer much hardship, but you will restore me to life again
and lift me up from the depths of the earth. You will restore me to even
greater honor and comfort me once again.

PSALM 71:20–21 NLT

Worldly pleasures bring a temporary comfort, but the problem still remains when the pleasure or comfort fades. However, the words of God are soothing and provide permanent hope and peace. Through God's Word, you will be changed, and your troubles will dim in the bright light of Christ.

*T*hank You, Father, for the rich comfort Your Word provides. Help me to remember to find my comfort in scripture rather than through earthly things. Amen.

· ·

Depend on the LORD and his strength; always go to him for help.

PSALM 105:4 NCV

The Spirit of God, who raised Jesus from the dead, lives in you. And just as God raised Christ Jesus from the dead, he will give life to your mortal bodies by this same Spirit living within you.

ROMANS 8:11 NLT

It's natural to want to do things on our own. We all want to be independent and strong. But there's another way. Our heavenly Father wants to help. Whatever we face—wherever we go—whatever dreams we have for our lives, we can take courage and know that anything is possible when we draw on the power of God.

Father, help me to remember that You are always with me, ready to help me do all things. Amen.

Day 116
WORSHIP

*Because of your great mercy, I come to your house, LORD, and I am filled
with wonder as I bow down to worship at your holy temple.*

PSALM 5:7 CEV

*All the earth shall worship thee, and shall sing unto thee;
they shall sing to thy name. Selah.*

PSALM 66:4 KJV

Only God is worthy to be praised. In all we do and all we are, our lives should pay
tribute to God. Nothing else is good enough. Offer God worship and praise, for He
alone is deserving.

*Thank You for the gifts You give, almighty God. From the rising of the sun to its setting
in the night, I will praise You for all that You have done. Glory is Yours, Father. Amen.*

REFLECTING CHRIST

*We are therefore Christ's ambassadors, as though God were making his appeal
through us. We implore you on Christ's behalf: Be reconciled to God.*

2 CORINTHIANS 5:20 NIV

*"I will make you a light for all nations to show people all over
the world the way to be saved."*

ISAIAH 49:6 NCV

We are called to be Christ's representatives, His ambas-sadors. Humility, not
arrogance, should be observed in our lives. Forgiveness and love should be readily
displayed. Peace should shine forth. When nonbelievers observe your life, do they
receive an accurate picture of Jesus?

*Dear Lord, help me realize the responsibility I have as Your ambassador. May I
correctly represent You to others so that they will be drawn to You. Amen.*

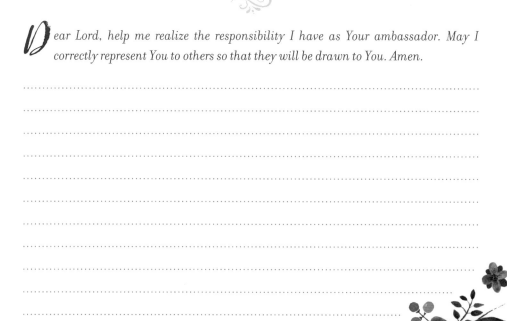

Day 118
GOD'S PROTECTION

But the Lord is my defence; and my God is the rock of my refuge.

PSALM 94:22 KJV

Those who live in the shelter of the Most High will find rest in the shadow of the Almighty. This I declare about the Lord: he alone is my refuge, my place of safety; he is my God, and I trust him.

PSALM 91:1–2 NLT

If you are abiding in Christ, moment by moment, you are constantly safe under His protection. In that secret place, that hidden place in Him, you can maintain holy serenity, a peace of mind that surpasses all understanding. If you are trusting in God, nothing can move you or harm you.

God, You are my Refuge. Your Word is the truth on which I rely. Amen.

Lazy people want much but get little, but those who work hard will prosper.

PROVERBS 13:4 NLT

A heart at peace gives life to the body, but envy rots the bones.

PROVERBS 14:30 NIV

If ambition means wanting to do well at your job, then ambition is good. But if ambition means you want to compete against your neighbor, destroy his reputation, and rejoice when you do better than your colleague does, then ambition is destructive.

Lord, help my only ambition to be to do my best and to become like You. Amen.

Day 120
BLESSINGS

*Those who live to please the Spirit will harvest everlasting life from the Spirit.
So let's not get tired of doing what is good. At just the right time we
will reap a harvest of blessing if we don't give up.*

GALATIANS 6:8–9 NLT

*"I am coming to you now, but I say these things while I am still in the world,
so that they may have the full measure of my joy within them."*

JOHN 17:13 NIV

God longs to bestow His richest blessings on us. He loves us, so He desires to fill our cup to overflowing with the things that He knows will bring us pleasure and growth. You may not even realize it, but perhaps your actions dictate that your cup remain half-empty. Seek a full cup and enjoy the full measure of the joy of the Lord.

*Dear Jesus, forgive me for not accepting the fullness of Your blessings and Your joy.
Help me to see the ways that I prevent my cup from being filled to overflowing. Amen.*

....
....
....
....
....
....
....
....
....
....

For even when we were with you, we used to give you this order: if anyone is not willing to work, then he is not to eat, either. For we hear that some among you are leading an undisciplined life, doing no work at all, but acting like busybodies.

2 Thessalonians 3:10–11 nasb

Who can find a virtuous and capable wife? She is more precious than rubies. . . . She is energetic and strong, a hard worker.

Proverbs 31:10, 17 nlt

Our attitudes and actions on the job speak volumes to those around us. Although it may be tempting to do just enough to get by, we put forth our best effort when we remember we represent God to the world. A Christian's character on the job should be a positive reflection of the Lord.

Father, help me to represent You well through my work. I want to reflect Your love in all I do. Amen.

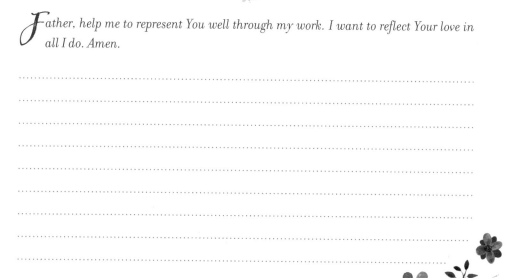

Day 122
TERRORISM

....

Do justice to the fatherless and the oppressed,
so that man who is of the earth may strike terror no more.

PSALM 10:18 ESV

In righteousness shalt thou be established: thou shalt be far from oppression;
for thou shalt not fear: and from terror; for it shall not come near thee.

ISAIAH 54:14 KJV

Today terrorism is a real fear that often threatens to overwhelm us. No matter what we experience, nothing is larger than God. He protects and encourages us, just as He calls the terrorist to give up his ways and turn instead to Him.

Heavenly Father, it's hard to take in all the horrific things that happen in this life. Keep my eyes focused on You. Amen.

*Giving to the poor will keep you from poverty, but if you close your eyes
to their needs, everyone will curse you.*

PROVERBS 28:27 CEV

*Whoever oppresses the poor to increase his own wealth,
or gives to the rich, will only come to poverty.*

PROVERBS 22:16 ESV

Contrary to popular belief, the poor have not been deserted by God. He often uses people to help supply the impoverished person's needs and calls on Christians to aid those who lack money.

L ord, use me to help those who are struggling. Turn my selfishness to love for others, that I might share what I have been given. Amen.

Day 124
WORRY

. . . .

"Don't be like this people, always afraid somebody is plotting against them.
Don't fear what they fear. Don't take on their worries."

Isaiah 8:12 msg

Give all your worries and cares to God, for he cares about you.

1 Peter 5:7 nlt

Give Christ your concerns, worries, what-ifs. Put all those cares on Him, for His shoulders are broad enough to carry them. And the amazing thing is that He actually wants them!

God, I come to You today with all my burdens. They are rolling off my shoulders and onto Yours. Thank You for sharing Your strength. Amen.

. . . .

. . . .

. . . .

. . . .

. . . .

. . . .

. . . .

. . . .

. . . .

. . . .

. . . .

. . . .

. . . .

Don't trust in money you have taken from others. Don't put false hope in things you have stolen. Even if your riches grow, don't put your trust in them.

PSALM 62:10 NIrV

But don't forget to help others and to share your possessions with them. This too is like offering a sacrifice that pleases God.

HEBREWS 13:16 CEV

Money cannot buy happiness, nor can it bring us life. Christ brings us life, and He brings it most abundantly. He is the real treasure, and as long as our hearts remain with Him, our lives will truly be rich.

Help me to keep my eyes focused on Your truth, Lord. Enable me to show others that You are the real treasure in life. Amen.

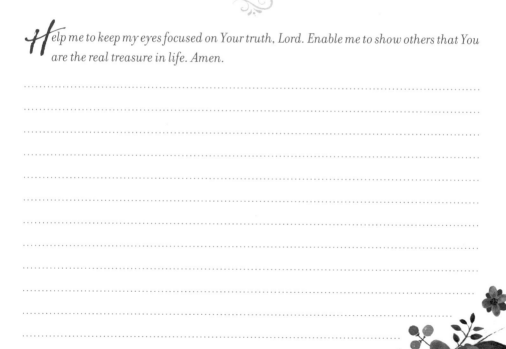

Day 126
JUSTICE

....

Your righteousness is like the mighty mountains, your justice like the ocean depths.
You care for people and animals alike, O Lord.

PSALM 36:6 NLT

And the word of the Lord came again to Zechariah: "This is what the Lord Almighty said:
'Administer true justice; show mercy and compassion to one another. Do not oppress the
widow or the fatherless, the foreigner or the poor. Do not plot evil against each other.' "

ZECHARIAH 7:8–10 NIV

Our object lesson in justice is the cross, for through it, the Father exacted justice for the sins of the world. Jesus was punished for our sins to make us right with our loving Father. We must pass justice on to others as it has been given to us.

Father, when I am tempted to be unfair, bring me to the cross. You have paid the price.
Amen!

....
....
....
....
....
....
....
....
....
....
....

"I have done the Lord's work humbly and with many tears. I have endured the trials that came to me from the plots of the Jews."

ACTS 20:19 NLT

Keep your eyes on Jesus, who both began and finished this race we're in.

HEBREWS 12:2 MSG

In the face of trouble, we often try to run away, or we turn to worldly solutions. These can never be enough. Instead, we must turn to God and rely on His strength to get us through. He is greater than any trial this world can produce.

O Lord, receive me into Your loving care. Help me to place You, and You alone, at the center of my life. Amen.

Day 128
FAITH

. . . .

Let love and faithfulness never leave you; bind them around your neck,
write them on the tablet of your heart.

PROVERBS 3:3 NIV

But you cannot make God accept you because of something you do.
God accepts sinners only because they have faith in him.

ROMANS 4:5 CEV

If we will learn to accept a God who is greater and more powerful than the limits our minds can grasp, we will begin to experience God more fully. Faith is not without reason, but it is always beyond reason.

Help me, Father, to accept what I do not understand, to believe that which I cannot see, and to trust that which is beyond my comprehension. Amen.

. . . .
. . . .
. . . .
. . . .
. . . .
. . . .
. . . .
. . . .
. . . .
. . . .
. . . .

*So that you may live a life worthy of the Lord and please him in every way:
bearing fruit in every good work, growing in the knowledge of God.*

COLOSSIANS 1:10 NIV

"A good tree cannot bear bad fruit, and a bad tree cannot bear good fruit."

MATTHEW 7:18 NIV

How people spend their time and money, how much they help the needy, whether they are patient when wronged, whether they gossip. . .every action bears fruit, revealing whether individuals are true disciples of Jesus Christ. The lives we lead shout whether Christ is front and center in our lives.

ord, may my every action bear witness of Your Holy Spirit's work, leading people to a direct knowledge of the truth. Amen.

Day 130
FEARING GOD

"Oh, that they had such a heart in them that they would fear Me and always keep all My commandments, that it might be well with them and with their children forever!"

DEUTERONOMY 5:29 NKJV

"And now, Israel, what does the LORD your God require of you, but to fear the LORD your God, to walk in all His ways and to love Him, to serve the LORD your God with all your heart and with all your soul?"

DEUTERONOMY 10:12 NKJV

Why does the Bible say we should "fear" God? In reality, to fear God is not the same as fearing the creepy-crawly spider inching up the living room wall. Instead, we fear God when we have a deep respect and reverence for Him.

Lord, help my daily actions and speech to reflect my respect for You. Amen.

And forgive us our sins; for we also forgive every one that is indebted to us.
And lead us not into temptation; but deliver us from evil.

LUKE 11:4 KJV

"For if you forgive other people when they sin against you, your heavenly Father will also forgive you. But if you do not forgive others their sins, your Father will not forgive your sins."

MATTHEW 6:14–15 NIV

Sometimes we struggle to forgive a careless or hurtful remark. In the Sermon on the Mount, Jesus encouraged His listeners to forgive offenders, but He didn't mention whether the offenders sought forgiveness. Jesus was only concerned about believers' obligations. We forgive because we are forgiven!

Lord, how often I ask You for forgiveness—and how readily You give it. May I never take for granted the gift of Your forgiveness. Amen.

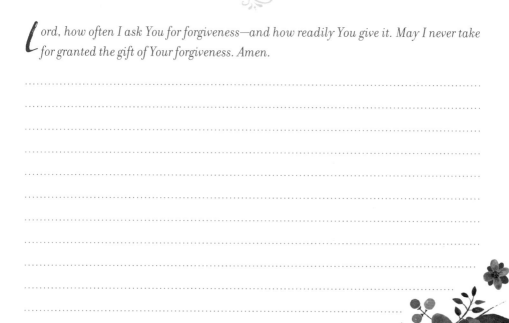

Day 132
FAITH

But without faith it is impossible to please him: for he that cometh to God must believe that he is, and that he is a rewarder of them that diligently seek him.

Hebrews 11:6 KJV

But that no man is justified by the law in the sight of God, it is evident: for, The just shall live by faith.

Galatians 3:11 KJV

It has been said that faith is the bird that sings to greet the dawn while it is still dark. Faith assures us that daylight will dawn in our darkest moments, affirming God's presence so that even when positive feelings fade, our moods surrender to song.

Heavenly Father, I desire my faith, not my emotions, to dictate my life. I pray for balance in my hide-under-the-covers days, so that I might surrender to You in song. Amen.

"For as churning cream produces butter, and as twisting the nose produces blood, so stirring up anger produces strife."

PROVERBS 30:33 NIV

Abram said to Lot, "Let's not have fighting between us, between your shepherds and my shepherds. After all, we're family. Look around. Isn't there plenty of land out there? Let's separate. If you go left, I'll go right; if you go right, I'll go left."

GENESIS 13:8–9 MSG

When faced with disagreements, do we dig our feet into the ground and refuse to budge? Or do we put our desires second? Much bitterness among Christians could be avoided if we said, "You choose first. I will accept your decision."

eavenly Father, You have adopted us into Your family. Teach us to live together as brothers and sisters, united in Your love. Amen.

. . . .

. . . .

. . . .

. . . .

. . . .

. . . .

. . . .

. . . .

. . . .

. . . .

Day 134
STRENGTH

Our Lord, you break the bows of warriors, but you give strength to everyone who stumbles.

1 Samuel 2:4 cev

Goodness and fairness will give him strength, like a belt around his waist.

Isaiah 11:5 ncv

When you don't think you can take another step—don't! Just hold on. Tomorrow will give you a fresh start and the strength you need to go a little further and hold on a little longer. You've gotten this far in your faith believing that God will keep His promises and help you reach your destination.

Lord, help me to hold fast to You. With You by my side, I can make it through all circumstances of life no matter how tough they seem. Amen.

*People of Israel, what does the LORD your God want from you? The LORD wants you
to respect and follow him, to love and serve him with all your heart and soul.*

DEUTERONOMY 10:12 CEV

"God will show his mercy forever and ever to those who worship and serve him."

LUKE 1:50 NCV

As we go about our day, doing whatever exciting or mundane activities we do, it is
easy to lose focus and forget that our first priority is to serve God. In each action, our
service and attitudes can reflect Christ—the Beginning and the End.

*G*od, help me to serve You in all I do. Amen.

Day 136
WEALTH

"I love those who love me; and those who diligently seek me will find me. Riches and honor are with me, enduring wealth and righteousness. My fruit is better than gold, even pure gold, and my yield better than choicest silver."

PROVERBS 8:17–19 NASB

Command those who are rich in this present world not to be arrogant nor to put their hope in wealth, which is so uncertain, but to put their hope in God, who richly provides us with everything for our enjoyment.

1 TIMOTHY 6:17 NIV

God desires to bless us with possessions we can enjoy. But it displeases Him when we strain to attain riches in a worldly manner. Riches are uncertain, but faith in God to meet our needs is indicative of the pure in heart.

Heavenly Father, my hope is in You for my needs. I surrender my desire to attain earthly wealth. May I be rich in godliness and righteousness. Amen.

*Do not let sin control the way you live; do not give in to sinful desires. . . .
Instead, give yourselves completely to God, for you were dead, but now you
have new life. . . . Sin is no longer your master. Instead,
you live under the freedom of God's grace.*

ROMANS 6:12–14 NLT

I have no greater joy than to hear that my children are walking in the truth.

3 JOHN 1:4 NIV

While we remain on earth, sin easily tempts us. Our hearts are more prone to wander
than we'd like to admit. That's just why believers must continually resist sin's hold
and draw near to Jesus. He has opened the doors of forgiveness for every believer
who habitually confesses the sticky sin that pulls him or her away from God.

Cleanse me, Lord, from the goop of sin, and help me stick to You alone. Amen.

Day 138
APPEARANCE

*We are not commending ourselves to you again but giving you cause to boast about us,
so that you may be able to answer those who boast about outward
appearance and not about what is in the heart.*

2 Corinthians 5:12 esv

*"Whenever you fast, do not put on a gloomy face as the hypocrites do, for they neglect
their appearance so that they will be noticed by men when they are fasting.
Truly I say to you, they have their reward in full."*

Matthew 6:16 nasb

Remembering that God sees within, that we are called to be attractive from within because of Him, is never easy. Worldly standards of beauty change; God's standards never do. It is not our makeup but what we are made of that lets our true beauty shine.

Lord, let my heart and manner represent You as best I can. Amen.

For wisdom is more precious than rubies, and nothing you desire can compare with her.

PROVERBS 8:11 NIV

*Who is wise and understanding among you? Let them show it by their good life,
by deeds done in the humility that comes from wisdom.*

JAMES 3:13 NIV

Wisdom. The very term sounds outdated. But biblical wisdom, crafted by God before the earth existed, remains as fresh and powerful as its Creator. Whoever heeds God's instruction gains more than silver, gold, or rubies. His truth, His directions lead listeners to new life.

*F*ather, *help us shake off the hypnotizing effects of the culture's values and listen to Your wisdom. Amen.*

Day 140
KINDNESS

....

Your kindness and love will always be with me each day of my life,
and I will live forever in your house, LORD.

PSALM 23:6 CEV

Do not let kindness and truth leave you; bind them around your neck,
write them on the tablet of your heart.

PROVERBS 3:3 NASB

Satan delights when we treat others in an unkind manner. However, God, upon request, will help us prioritize our commitments so that our *yes* means *yes* and our *no* means *no*. Then in everything we do, we are liberated to do to others as we would have them do to us.

L ord, enable me in everything to do to others as I would desire for them to do to me. Amen.

....
....
....
....
....
....
....
....
....
....
....
....

Fear not, little flock; for it is your Father's good pleasure to give you the kingdom.

LUKE 12:32 KJV

But whoso hearkeneth unto me shall dwell safely, and shall be quiet from fear of evil.

PROVERBS 1:33 KJV

When you become bewildered and petrified by fear, "don't be afraid. Just stand still and watch the LORD rescue you today" (Exodus 14:13 NLT.) Be persistent, and God will see you through.

ord, be my shield. Surround me with Your presence. Help me to keep still in this situation and watch You see me through it. And I will praise You forever and ever, in Jesus' name. Amen.

Day 142
PRAISE

You are the living LORD! I will praise you!

2 SAMUEL 22:47 CEV

Why, my soul, are you downcast? Why so disturbed within me?
Put your hope in God, for I will yet praise him, my Savior and my God.

PSALM 42:11 NIV

Imagine how God feels when one of His children praises Him simply for who He is, even when circumstances are far from perfect. Don't you suppose it feels like a tight hug around His neck? Praise God regardless. Praise Him yet, as the psalmists did. Adore Him today, for He is God.

Father, You are the great I AM, faithful and good. I adore You. I choose to praise You whether You alter my circumstances or not. Amen.

The Lord answered, "I can do anything! Watch and you'll see my words come true."

NUMBERS 11:23 CEV

Jesus answered and said to him, "If anyone loves Me, he will keep My word;
and My Father will love him, and We will come to him and make Our home with him."

JOHN 14:23 NKJV

Words of anger, frustration, confusion, and jealousy take away from the spirit of man, but words of affirmation and gestures of kindness add to every heart. Consider your words before you speak. Will you be adding to or taking away from that person with what you are about to say?

God, help me to think before I speak so that I can have a positive influence on others. Amen.

. . . .

. . . .

. . . .

. . . .

. . . .

. . . .

. . . .

. . . .

. . . .

. . . .

. . . .

. . . .

. . . .

Day 144
JUDGING

Don't judge others, and God won't judge you. Don't be hard on others,
and God won't be hard on you.

LUKE 6.37 CEV

"For you will be treated as you treat others. The standard you use in judging
is the standard by which you will be judged."

MATTHEW 7:2 NLT

Leaping to judgment. Many churchgoers fall into this trap. Standing near God, an unbeliever may come to faith—if the people in His congregation are loving and nurturing. We need not judge a casual acquaintance's spiritual life—God can do that. All we need to do is love, and He will bring blessings.

Thank You, Lord, that Your first reaction to me was love, not condemnation. Turn my heart in love to all who don't yet know You. Amen.

God's word is alive and working and is sharper than a double-edged sword.
It cuts all the way into us, where the soul and the spirit are joined, to the center
of our joints and bones. And it judges the thoughts and feelings in our hearts.

HEBREWS 4:12 NCV

God's kingdom isn't just a lot of words. It is power.

1 CORINTHIANS 4:20 CEV

A journey through the holy scriptures can be a thrilling experience. To hear the stories of God and His people is a joy.

Indeed, Lord, You are great. Teach me new things every day from Your Word. Amen.

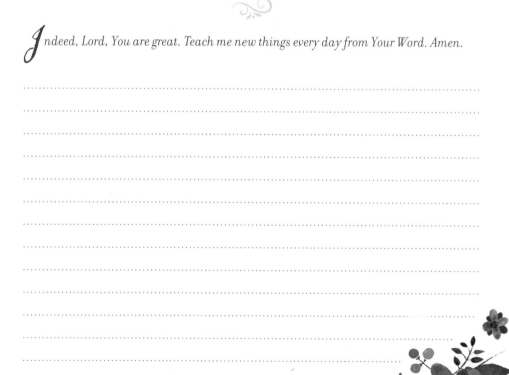

Day 146
LOVING OTHERS

The Lord has told you, human, what is good; he has told you what he wants from you: to do what is right to other people, love being kind to others.

MICAH 6:8 NCV

The Lord watches over those who do what is right. But he hates sinful people and those who love to hurt others.

PSALM 11:5 NIrV

Our duty as Christians is to look at all individuals as equals, brothers and sisters whom we can reach out to. When we look down on others, we do not just withdraw our reach from them, but from Christ as well.

Dear Jesus, help me to see Your Spirit in all people I meet. Teach me to love those around me as You would love them. Amen.

"They will never again pollute themselves with their idols and vile images and rebellion, for I will save them from their sinful apostasy. I will cleanse them. Then they will truly be my people, and I will be their God."

EZEKIEL 37:23 NLT

Return, ye backsliding children, and I will heal your backslidings. Behold, we come unto thee; for thou art the LORD our God.

JEREMIAH 3:22 KJV

Though God calls His people to a lifetime commitment to Him, sin so easily distracts us from our goal. But even as we're pulled away from Him by the lures of Satan, God calls us to return to Him and love Him with an undivided heart.

Father, so often I stray from You. Guide me back to Your side, that I might love You above all. Amen.

Day 148
GOD'S PROVISION

The young lions do lack, and suffer hunger:
but they that seek the Lord shall not want any good thing.

PSALM 34:10 KJV

He hath given meat unto them that fear him: he will ever be mindful of his covenant.

PSALM 111:5 KJV

God's providence is revealed in both the big and small: the timing of a call from a friend, the helping hand of a coworker, the cheer of a sunny day. There are no coincidences—just a loving God revealing Himself to those who watch for Him.

Loving God, remind me to watch for You in daily life. Help me to see You in people, nature, and circumstances. Amen.

Be not forgetful to entertain strangers:
for thereby some have entertained angels unawares.

HEBREWS 13:2 KJV

Use hospitality one to another without grudging.

1 PETER 4:9 KJV

Living lavishly doesn't mean the same thing to everyone. But in most cultures, lavish living best translates as hospitality. Welcoming next-door neighbors, coworkers, family, and friends gives Christians the God-ordained privilege to live lavishly by extending genuine hospitality.

Father, thank You for all that You've given me. Thank You for the privilege of encouraging others with something as simple as a genuine welcome. Amen.

Day 150
REGRET

....

When the Lord blesses you with riches, you have nothing to regret.

PROVERBS 10:22 CEV

For now we see only a reflection as in a mirror; then we shall see face to face.
Now I know in part; then I shall know fully, even as I am fully known.

1 CORINTHIANS 13:12 NIV

We don't have to look back with regret. We can live today with tomorrow in mind. We can gain spiritual wisdom by keeping our eyes on the Lord today. Let today count for eternity!

ear Lord, help me to live today in light of eternity. May Your will be done in my life today. Amen.

*They gave up the truth about God for a lie, and they worshiped God's
creation instead of God, who will be praised forever. Amen.*

ROMANS 1:25 CEV

*"You will go out in joy and be led forth in peace; the mountains and hills will burst
into song before you, and all the trees of the field will clap their hands."*

ISAIAH 55:12 NIV

We don't have to be outdoorsy to appreciate and be inspired by the wonders of God's
creation. Wildflowers that grow alongside highways or the cloud formations that
dance in the sky inspire us to praise God, the creator of all things. Nature declares
the glory of the Lord.

Lord, the beauty in Your creation inspires me to sing Your praises. Praise be to God. Amen.

Day 152
SPIRITUAL GROWTH

....

We're waiting the arrival of the Savior, the Master, Jesus Christ, who will transform our earthy bodies into glorious bodies like his own. He'll make us beautiful and whole with the same powerful skill by which he is putting everything as it should be, under and around him.

PHILIPPIANS 3:20–21 MSG

You have now become a new person and are always learning more about Christ. You are being made more like Christ. He is the One Who made you.

COLOSSIANS 3:10 NLV

No one likes to hear negative comments, whether they are true or not. It takes a special person to seek criticism and suggestions for improvement. The Bible says that we should be humble and always trying to improve ourselves.

O Lord, help me to be open to the comments of others. Let me face my shortcomings with dignity and open-mindedness. Amen.

....

....

....

....

....

....

....

....

....

....

DECISION MAKING

*Mark well that G*OD *doesn't miss a move you make; he's aware of every step you take.*
The shadow of your sin will overtake you; you'll find yourself stumbling all
over yourself in the dark. Death is the reward of an undisciplined
life; your foolish decisions trap you in a dead end.

PROVERBS 5:21–23 MSG

For as many as are led by the Spirit of God, these are sons of God.

ROMANS 8:14 NKJV

God has the whole world in His hands, but daily choices belong to you. Choose to live in His will, making decisions based on His direction. Knowing His will comes from a personal relationship and from time spent with Him in prayer and in the Word.

*H*eavenly Father, I choose Your dream, Your destiny for my life. Help me to make the right choices for my life as I follow You. Amen.

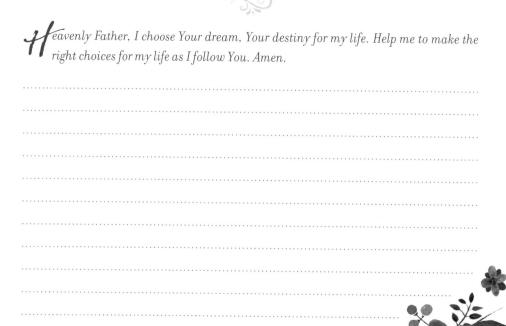

Day 154
TEMPTATION

Brethren, even if anyone is caught in any trespass, you who are spiritual, restore such a one in a spirit of gentleness; each one looking to yourself, so that you too will not be tempted.

GALATIANS 6:1 NASB

Run from temptations that capture young people. Always do the right thing. Be faithful, loving, and easy to get along with. Worship with people whose hearts are pure.

2 TIMOTHY 2:22 CEV

Sin can quickly get a foothold in our lives. Beware of your temptations. Know your areas of vulnerability and avoid them. Draw close to the Lord. Allow Him to satisfy your deepest longings. When we cling to good, evil loses its grip.

D ear Lord, help me avoid temptation. May I draw close to You so I can cling to good and avoid evil in my life. Amen.

....

....

....

....

....

....

....

....

....

....

....

For if our heart condemn us, God is greater than our heart, and knoweth all things.

1 John 3:20 kjv

So I confessed my sins and told them all to you. I said, "I'll tell the Lord each one of my sins." Then you forgave me and took away my guilt.

Psalm 32:5 cev

The apostle Paul's example shows the effect a clear conscience can have in the life of a believer. Boldness! Boldness to live for Christ. Obedience, readily confessing sin, and total reliance on God to replace that sin with righteous living help create a clear conscience.

Holy Spirit, reveal to me my sin, cleanse me, and empower me to walk obediently with a clear conscience that I might live boldly and courageously for You. Amen.

Day 156
DATING

Do not be unequally yoked together with unbelievers. For what fellowship has righteousness with lawlessness? And what communion has light with darkness?

2 Corinthians 6.14 nkjv

"But those who are considered worthy to attain to that age and to the resurrection from the dead neither marry nor are given in marriage."

Luke 20:35 esv

Loving families are part of God's earthly plan. But whether we are single or wed, our ultimate goal remains the same: to serve our Lord, not just a spouse. Married or single, you can do God's will. Just love Him best. That's all He asks.

Lord, You love me just as I am. Make my life a witness to You. Amen.

How blessed is the man who has made the LORD his trust, and has not turned to the proud, nor to those who lapse into falsehood.

PSALM 40:4 NASB

Believers in humble circumstances ought to take pride in their high position. But the rich should take pride in their humiliation—since they will pass away like a wild flower.

JAMES 1:9–10 NIV

Pride is a dangerous sin that separates us from our all-powerful God. When we focus on our own frail "power," we cannot truly see Him as Lord.

Lord, when I turn my attention inward, I lose sight of who You want me to be. Redirect my focus, please. Amen.

Day 158
ADVERSITY

So we may boldly say: "The LORD is my helper; I will not fear.
What can man do to me?"

HEBREWS 13:6 NKJV

Anyone who meets a testing challenge head-on and manages to stick it out is mighty
fortunate. For such persons loyally in love with God, the reward is life and more life.

JAMES 1:12 MSG

Scripture overflows with stories of God's beloved children undergoing extreme hardships. Just because we have faith, hope, and trust in the Lord does not mean that life will be easy. Instead, God's love for us means that He will provide a way through, not around, adversity, resulting in His greater glory.

Father God, I know that no matter how troubled my life is, You can provide me a way
to persevere. Help me to trust Your guidance and love. Amen.

....
....
....
....
....
....
....
....
....
....
....

Your faith will be like gold that has been tested in a fire. And these trials will prove that your faith is worth much more than gold that can be destroyed. They will show that you will be given praise and honor and glory when Jesus Christ returns.

1 Peter 1:7 cev

These things I have spoken unto you, that in me ye might have peace. In the world ye shall have tribulation: but be of good cheer; I have overcome the world.

John 16:33 kjv

Expect trouble, but refuse to let it defeat you. Trials strengthen our faith and our character. No one gets excited about a trial, yet we can be assured that God is still in control even when trouble comes our way.

Lord Jesus, be my strength as I face trouble in this life. Walk with me. Hold my hand. Assure me that in my weakness, You are strong. Amen.

Day 160
GOSSIP

A froward man soweth strife: and a whisperer separateth chief friends.

PROVERBS 16:28 KJV

Do not pay attention to every word people say, or you may hear your servant cursing you—for you know in your heart that many times you yourself have cursed others.

ECCLESIASTES 7:21–22 NIV

In an ideal world, no one would speak badly of us, and we would never gossip about someone else. But in the real world, it happens. The best defense against hurt feelings is an intentional ignorance. The next time you overhear your name, keep walking.

Lord, teach me to put a guard on both my lips and my ears. Close my ears to gossip that swirls around me. Amen.

....

....

....

....

....

....

....

....

....

....

....

....

When Job prayed for his friends, the LORD restored his fortunes.
In fact, the LORD gave him twice as much as before!

JOB 42:10 NLT

There are "friends" who destroy each other, but a real friend sticks closer than a brother.

PROVERBS 18:24 NLT

Jesus sticks close by us at our most undesirable, least lovable moments. We can tell Him anything and He understands. Like a true friend, Jesus enhances our good qualities and, with a breath of kindness, blows the rest away.

Dear Jesus, thank You for loving me even when I fail, encouraging me in my discouragement, and sticking close to me during tough times. May I be as good a friend as You are. Amen.

Day 162
SPIRITUAL REFRESHMENT

Though I walk in the midst of trouble, thou wilt revive me.

Psalm 138:7 KJV

You're my place of quiet retreat; I wait for your Word to renew me.

Psalm 119:114 MSG

There are many times when we find ourselves so starved spiritually that we take and take and take but give little back. God understands that, and He knows that by feeding us when we hunger, we are being strengthened to give to others later on.

Forgive me for the times when I take without offering anything in return. Amen.

Let the wise hear and increase in learning,
and the one who understands obtain guidance.

PROVERBS 1:5 ESV

May the Lord direct your hearts into the love of God and into the steadfastness of Christ.

2 THESSALONIANS 3:5 NASB

Even before Jesus sent His Holy Spirit to indwell believers, God used a variety of means to guide His people. Praise be to God for giving us His Spirit, who resides in us so that we need never lose our direction as we navigate our way through life.

Thank You, Jesus, for sending Your Holy Spirit to lead me in the right direction. Amen.

Day 164
ETERNITY

. . . .

"My sheep hear My voice, and I know them, and they follow Me. And I give them eternal life, and they shall never perish; neither shall anyone snatch them out of My hand."

JOHN 10:27–28 NKJV

So just as sin ruled over all people and brought them to death, now God's wonderful grace rules instead, giving us right standing with God and resulting in eternal life through Jesus Christ our Lord.

ROMANS 5:21 NLT

Jesus came to give us eternal life in heaven as well as abundant life on earth. As we allow His Word to speak to our hearts, we grow in our relationship with Him and assurance of eternal life to come.

Dear Lord, help me to pursue my relationship with You now. May I know You more with each passing day so that I will be excited when we meet face-to-face. Amen.

. . . .

. . . .

. . . .

. . . .

. . . .

. . . .

. . . .

. . . .

. . . .

. . . .

The generous soul will be made rich, and he who waters will also be watered himself.

PROVERBS 11:25 NKJV

The generous will themselves be blessed, for they share their food with the poor.

PROVERBS 22:9 NIV

Christ asks each one of us where it is we keep our treasure. Is it on earth or is it in heaven? Surely, God wants every person to enjoy life and to share in good times, but He does not find joy in the celebration of a few when many suffer.

O heavenly Father, open my eyes to the needs of those around me. Help me to share the blessings that I have been given. Amen.

Day 166
GOD'S WILL

And do not be conformed to this world, but be transformed by the renewing of your mind, so that you may prove what the will of God is, that which is good and acceptable and perfect.

ROMANS 12:2 NASB

I urge, then, first of all, that petitions, prayers, intercession and thanksgiving be made for all people. . . .This is good, and pleases God our Savior, who wants all people to be saved and to come to a knowledge of the truth.

1 TIMOTHY 2:1, 3–4 NIV

Embracing God's love enables us to submit to His will. God not only loves us immensely, but He desires to bless us abundantly. However, from our human perspective, those spiritual blessings may be disguised. That is why we must cling to truth. We must believe that His will is perfect.

*D*ear Lord, may I rest secure in Your unconditional love. Enable me to trust You more. May I desire that Your will be done in my life. Amen.

ENCOURAGEMENT

May our Lord Jesus Christ himself and God our Father encourage you and strengthen you in every good thing you do and say. God loved us, and through his grace he gave us a good hope and encouragement that continues forever.

2 Thessalonians 2:16–17 ncv

And let us consider how we may spur one another on toward love and good deeds.

Hebrews 10:24 niv

We all need encouragement, but we all must learn to give encouragement as well. We also must rely on our brothers and sisters; if we encourage them, we believe that they, in turn, will encourage us.

ord, please help me to encourage others toward love and good deeds. Please also raise up brothers and sisters who will encourage me. Amen.

Day 168
COMFORT

*Christ encourages you, and his love comforts you. God's Spirit unites you,
and you are concerned for others.*

PHILIPPIANS 2:1 CEV

*And God shall wipe away all tears from their eyes; and there shall be no more death,
neither sorrow, nor crying, neither shall there be any more pain:
for the former things are passed away.*

REVELATION 21:4 KJV

The Holy Spirit is often called the Comforter because He comes alongside us and helps us to live out our daily faith. But throughout scripture, God also promises to comfort those who suffer affliction and hardship. We are not alone in the tough moments of our lives!

Lord, be with me this day. I need to feel You are near me, my Comforter. Amen.

SPIRITUAL GIFTS

For I say. . .to everyone who is among you, not to think of himself more highly than he ought to think, but to think soberly. . . .For as we have many members in one body, but all the members do not have the same function, so we are one body in Christ, and individually members of one another. Having then gifts differing according to the grace that is given to us, let us use them.

ROMANS 12:3–6 NKJV

This is why I remind you to fan into flames the spiritual gift God gave you when I laid my hands on you.

2 TIMOTHY 1:6 NLT

We need to awaken our latent gifts. Left unused, they lie dormant and neglected. Prayerfully seek ways to share your talents with those around you. Joy is yours when your gifts are used, and they are a blessing to those whom you have given them.

Father, help me to be a good steward of the gifts You have given me by using them creatively for others, igniting them to live for You. Amen.

Day 170
HARMONY

Now make me completely happy! Live in harmony by showing love for each other.
Be united in what you think, as if you were only one person.

PHILIPPIANS 2:2 CEV

Live in harmony with one another. Do not be haughty,
but associate with the lowly. Never be wise in your own sight.

ROMANS 12:16 ESV

Harmony with others isn't always easy. Differences can chafe at our patience. A willed choice of acting in love is needed instead of a rash response that may feel good at the time but will further divide. Only when peace is restored can believers experience how good and pleasant it is to dwell in unity.

*P*rince of Peace, help me to make unity my focus. Enable me to make every effort to preserve oneness with fellow believers. Then with one heart and one mouth we can glorify You. Amen.

*"I paid a huge price for you. . . . That's how much you mean to me! That's how much
I love you! I'd sell off the whole world to get you back, trade the creation just for you."*

ISAIAH 43:3–4 MSG

*Meanwhile, creation is confused, but not because it wants to be confused.
God made it this way in the hope that creation would be set free from
decay and would share in the glorious freedom of his children.*

ROMANS 8:20–21 CEV

We have been given life so that we may enjoy it. It is a gift from God. When we pursue
God and a deeper knowledge of His will, we are seeking a deeper understanding of all
creation.

*Through Your wisdom, Lord, I can hope to come to know the fullness of life and the
beauty of Your creation. I praise You in Your greatness, O Father. Amen.*

....

....

....

....

....

....

....

....

....

....

....

Day 172
WORRY

You will rest safe and secure, filled with hope and emptied of worry.

JOB 11:18 CEV

"And why do you worry about clothes? See how the flowers of the field grow.
They do not labor or spin. Yet I tell you that not even Solomon in
all his splendor was dressed like one of these."

MATTHEW 6:28–29 NIV

God knows that worries can easily overwhelm us. That's why He tells us not to worry and encourages us to trust in Him. When our concerns are in His hands, they are in the right place.

Father, this life provides an endless source of worry. Thank You for being the source of endless peace. I rest in Your care. Amen.

GOD'S PROTECTION

*And I looked, and arose and said to the nobles, to the leaders, and to the rest of the people,
"Do not be afraid of them. Remember the Lord, great and awesome, and fight for
your brethren, your sons, your daughters, your wives, and your houses."*

NEHEMIAH 4:14 NKJV

*But Moses told the people, "Don't be afraid. Just stand still and watch the LORD
rescue you today. The Egyptians you see today will never be seen again.
The LORD himself will fight for you. Just stay calm."*

EXODUS 14:13–14 NLT

Rest easy in the knowledge that God guides your steps. He will protect those who
put their trust in Him.

I need Your guiding love, almighty God. Thank You for Your continual protection. Amen.

Day 174
TRUTH

Blessed is the man to whom the Lord does not impute iniquity,
and in whose spirit there is no deceit.

PSALM 32:2 NKJV

God is not a man, that he should lie; neither the son of man, that he should repent:
hath he said, and shall he not do it? or hath he spoken, and shall he not make it good?

NUMBERS 23:19 KJV

Unlike the words of human beings, God's words can be trusted. What a comfort to know He who has promised us salvation, strength for daily living, and a glorious future means what He says!

Holy Lord, in a day when truth is hard to find, You won't change Your mind about me. Thank You! Amen.

So now we have a high priest who perfectly fits our needs:
completely holy, uncompromised by sin, with authority
extending as high as God's presence in heaven itself.

HEBREWS 7:26 MSG

"I am with you and will watch over you wherever you go, and I will bring you back
to this land. I will not leave you until I have done what I have promised you."

GENESIS 28:15 NIV

Only when we realize that God is with us every moment of every day are we compelled
to live good and upright lives. We must admit our weakness and that we need God to
motivate us when we will not motivate ourselves to right living.

*G*uide my steps, O Lord, that I might always, in every way, be found pleasing in Your
sight. Amen.

....

....

....

....

....

....

....

....

....

....

Day 176
DOUBT

....

My friends, watch out! Don't let evil thoughts or doubts make
any of you turn from the living God.

HEBREWS 3:12 CEV

Jesus said unto him, If thou canst believe, all things are possible to him that believeth.

MARK 9:23 KJV

Jesus Christ came that we might have a way to remove all doubt that God works all things for good. Christ assured us that God indeed watches over all people and that He reigns wisely and with justice.

O Lord of creation and love, You hear even my most quiet cry. Answer my every doubt with "I am." Amen.

PERFECTION

"Do you understand how he moves the clouds with wonderful perfection and skill?"

JOB 37:16 NLT

Nothing is completely perfect, except your teachings.
I deeply love your Law! I think about it all day.

PSALM 119:96–97 CEV

Perfection is not so perfect. Nothing is. We live in a flawed world no matter how much we work and strive. To love God's life-giving words is the closest we will ever come to achieving perfection here on earth.

Dear Lord, nothing is as important as following You. Please remind me of that when my quest for perfection overwhelms me. Amen.

Day 178
CHILDREN

....

Children's children are the crown of old men;
and the glory of children are their fathers.

PROVERBS 17:6 KJV

For the grace of God that bringeth salvation hath appeared to all men,
teaching us that, denying ungodliness and worldly lusts,
we should live soberly, righteously, and godly, in this present world.

TITUS 2:11–12 KJV

Godliness comes from within, from a deep desire to please and obey our Lord. It is developed in children by careful, consistent training. Children must learn to obey parents, first time, every time, so that their hearts are ready to obey Christ.

Father, give me the strength to do the hard job of consistently training my children in obedience. Let me give them a pattern of obedience to follow. Amen.

....
....
....
....
....
....
....
....
....
....
....

But I trust in your unfailing love; my heart rejoices in your salvation.

PSALM 13:5 NIV

*For I am not ashamed of the gospel, for it is the power of God for salvation
to everyone who believes, to the Jew first and also to the Greek.*

ROMANS 1:16 ESV

Like a lighthouse, true light, sent out through the clouds and darkness, can save lives.
A voice speaking the truth of Christ has real power behind it—the power of salvation.

*ord, let me reflect Your divine light, clearing away the fog and helping others come into
the safety of Your love. Amen.*

. . . .

. . . .

. . . .

. . . .

. . . .

. . . .

. . . .

. . . .

. . . .

. . . .

. . . .

. . . .

. . . .

. . . .

Day 180
STILLNESS

Meditate in your heart upon your bed, and be still.

PSALM 4:4 NASB

He says, "Be still, and know that I am God;
I will be exalted among the nations, I will be exalted in the earth."

PSALM 46:10 NIV

Stillness allows us to dwell on God's sovereignty, His goodness, and His deep love for us. He wants us to remember that He is God and that He is in control, regardless of our circumstances. Be still. . .and know that He is God.

God, so often I do all the talking. Quiet me before You now. Speak to my heart, I pray. Amen.

....
....
....
....
....
....
....
....
....
....
....
....

For as by the one man's disobedience the many were made sinners,
so by the one man's obedience the many will be made righteous.

ROMANS 5:19 ESV

But Samuel answered, "What pleases the LORD more: burnt offerings and sacrifices
or obedience to his voice? It is better to obey than to sacrifice.
It is better to listen to God than to offer the fat of sheep."

1 SAMUEL 15:22 NCV

Obedience is a long walk in the same direction. Flirtation with sin is like wandering in aimless circles. Each public or private action, no matter how large or small, plays a key role in moving you either toward or away from harmony in your relationship with God.

O Lord, help me live a life of integrity and moral purity, a no-compromise lifestyle in obedience to You. Amen.

Day 182
TRUST

*The instructions of the L*ORD *are perfect, reviving the soul.*
*The decrees of the L*ORD *are trustworthy, making wise the simple.*

PSALM 19:7 NLT

And we know that all things work together for good to them that love God,
to them who are the called according to his purpose.

ROMANS 8:28 KJV

God can and does use all things in our lives for His good purpose. It is easy to trust God when things are going well. And when we choose to trust Him in uncertain times, we receive a peace that gives us hope that sustains us. We are not disappointed, because God always keeps His promises. Our response is to trust Him.

L ord, may I trust You to fulfill Your purpose in my life. Amen.

I will listen to God the LORD. He has ordered peace for those who worship him.
Don't let them go back to foolishness.

PSALM 85:8 NCV

Don't fool yourself into thinking that you are a listener when you are anything but,
letting the Word go in one ear and out the other. Act on what you hear! Those who hear
and don't act are like those who glance in the mirror, walk away, and two minutes
later have no idea who they are, what they look like.

JAMES 1:22–24 MSG

So often we find ourselves tuning out the minister on Sunday morning or thinking about other things as we read our Bibles or sing hymns of praise. Our minds must be disciplined to really listen to God's Word. Then we must do the more difficult thing—act on what we've finally heard.

Dear Lord, please teach me to be attentive to Your Word. Help me to act on the things You teach me so that mine becomes a practical faith. Amen.

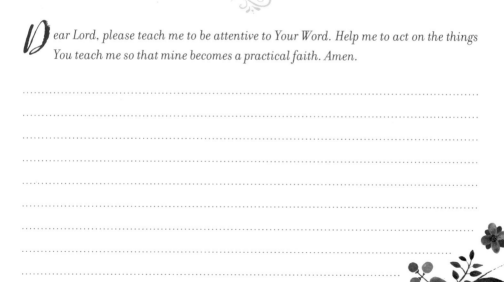

Day 184
CHANGE

God, who has ruled forever, will hear me and humble them.
For my enemies refuse to change their ways; they do not fear God.

PSALM 55:19 NLT

The LORD had said to Abram, "Leave your native country, your relatives, and your father's
family, and go to the land that I will show you. I will make you into a great nation.
I will bless you and make you famous, and you will be a blessing to others."

GENESIS 12:1–2 NLT

God wants us to be willing to embrace change that He brings into our lives. Even unbidden change. You may feel as if you're out on a limb, but don't forget that God is the tree trunk. He's not going to let you fall.

Holy, loving Father, in every area of my life, teach me to trust You more deeply. Amen.

....
....
....
....
....
....
....
....
....
....
....
....

LOVING OTHERS

"It is also true that we must love God with all our heart, mind, and strength, and that we must love others as much as we love ourselves. These commandments are more important than all the sacrifices and offerings that we could possibly make."

MARK 12:33 CEV

May the Lord make your love grow more and multiply for each other and for all people so that you will love others as we love you.

1 THESSALONIANS 3:12 NCV

We have been called by God to show love to everyone we come in contact with. We are even called to show love to those people that we will never meet. There are no shortcuts we can take. Love is a matter of giving everything we are, all the time.

Father, grant me a deeper knowledge of who You are. Fill me with an unselfish love. Amen.

....

....

....

....

....

....

....

....

....

....

....

....

Day 186
LOSS

But if the rest of the world's people were helped so much by Israel's sin and loss,
they will be helped even more by their full return.

ROMANS 11:12 CEV

Have mercy on me, my God, have mercy on me, for in you I take refuge.
I will take refuge in the shadow of your wings until the disaster has passed.

PSALM 57:1 NIV

God's Word is filled with promises of renewal and restoration. We may not see it today or next month or even ten years from now. Nevertheless, our Lord's name is Redeemer. He alone can and will redeem the valuable, the precious, and the everlastingly worthwhile.

Lord, when I'm overwhelmed by loss, draw me close to Your promises. Amen.

*Now mine eyes shall be open, and mine ears attent unto the prayer
that is made in this place.*

2 Chronicles 7:15 kjv

I will pray with the spirit, and I will also pray with the understanding.

1 Corinthians 14:15 nkjv

We need to see prayer as the greatest gift we can give, not as a last-ditch effort.
Promising that you will keep others in your prayers means that you will continue to
pray for them, without ceasing, until you hear of a resolution to their problem. "I'll
pray for you" are words that offer hope and life to people who are hurting.

*Dear Jesus, please forgive me for all the times I promised prayer in vain. Call to mind
the people I need to bring before Your throne each day. Amen.*

Day 188
BLESSINGS

Lord, you are mine! I promise to obey your words! With all my heart I want your blessings. Be merciful as you promised. I pondered the direction of my life, and I turned to follow your laws.

PSALM 119:57–59 NLT

Every good and perfect gift is from above, coming down from the Father of the heavenly lights, who does not change like shifting shadows.

JAMES 1:17 NIV

God is a gift giver. He is, in fact, the creator of all good gifts. He finds great joy in blessing you. The God who made you certainly knows your tastes and preferences. He even knows your favorites and your dreams. Most important, He knows your needs.

God, sometimes I am anxious. I want what I want, and I want it now. Calm my spirit and give me the patience to wait for Your perfect gifts. Amen.

It gave me great joy when some believers came and testified about your faithfulness to the truth, telling how you continue to walk in it.

3 John 1:3 niv

My dear brothers and sisters, I love you and want to see you. You bring me joy and make me proud of you, so stand strong in the Lord as I have told you.

Philippians 4:1 ncv

Being a Christian means so much more than just believing in the existence of Christ. Many people believe in Christ, but they consciously remove Him from their hearts and minds. As Christian people, we need to keep God close by us.

Be with me, O Lord. Plant Yourself firmly in my thoughts, and never let me turn from You. Amen.

Day 190
RIDICULE

*"You're blessed when your commitment to God provokes persecution.
The persecution drives you even deeper into God's kingdom."*

MATTHEW 5:10 MSG

*He who continually goes forth weeping, bearing seed for sowing,
shall doubtless come again with rejoicing, bringing his sheaves with him.*

PSALM 126:6 NKJV

With Jesus as our example, we can carry on, even when we're discouraged. Being belittled for our faith is tough, but we have hope, knowing what is to come. We can go out with seed for sowing, knowing there will come a time of great rejoicing.

Jesus, thank You for being the example I can follow. Help me to have the courage to face each day, knowing my joy is in You and my hope is in heaven. Amen.

SPIRITUAL GIFTS

The manifestation of the Spirit is given to each one for the profit of all: for to one is given the word of wisdom through the Spirit, to another the word of knowledge. . . to another faith . . . to another gifts of healings . . .to another the working of miracles, to another prophecy, to another discerning of spirits, to another different kinds of tongues, to another the interpretation of tongues. But one and the same Spirit works all these things.

1 Corinthians 12:7–11 nkjv

God has given each of you a gift from his great variety of spiritual gifts. Use them well to serve one another.

1 Peter 4:10 nlt

We should give of our gifts and talents because it is pleasing to God. God has given us many fine abilities, and it is important that we remember to use them for His service, not caring whether we receive praise.

I want to serve You freely and without letting my ego get in the way. Guide me in this pursuit. Amen.

Day 192
REFLECTING CHRIST

. . . .

Now when they saw the boldness of Peter and John, and perceived that
they were uneducated and untrained men, they marveled.
And they realized that they had been with Jesus

ACTS 4:13 NKJV

What I'm getting at, friends, is that you should simply keep on doing what you've done
from the beginning. . . . Be energetic in your life of salvation, reverent and sensitive
before God. That energy is God's energy, an energy deep within you, God himself
willing and working at what will give him the most pleasure.

PHILIPPIANS 2:12–13 MSG

When we meditate on scripture and seek the Lord in prayer regularly, we naturally become a little more like Him. May our lives undeniably reflect that we have been with the Son of God.

J esus, make me more like You today. Amen.

. . . .

. . . .

. . . .

. . . .

. . . .

. . . .

. . . .

. . . .

. . . .

And God has placed in the church first of all apostles, second prophets, third teachers, then miracles, then gifts of healing, of helping, of guidance, and of different kinds of tongues.

1 CORINTHIANS 12:28 NIV

When people do not accept divine guidance, they run wild. But whoever obeys the law is joyful.

PROVERBS 29:18 NLT

We would do best to become wise men and women, daily presenting ourselves to Jesus, asking Him to lead us on the right path. By following God's directions—in His Word, your quiet time, or conversations with others—you will be sure to stay on the right path and arrive safely home.

Jesus, I present myself to You. Show me the right path to walk with every step I take. Keep me away from evil and lead me to Your door. Amen.

Day 194
GOD'S PRESENCE

How we thank God for you! Because of you we have great joy as we enter God's presence.

1 Thessalonians 3:9 NLT

Am I a God at hand, saith the Lord, and not a God afar off? Can any hide himself
in secret places that I shall not see him? saith the Lord.
Do not I fill heaven and earth? saith the Lord.

Jeremiah 23:23–24 KJV

If the "sky is falling" or the sun is shining, do you still recognize the One who orders all the planets and all your days? Whether we see Him or not, God tells us He is there. And He's here, too—in the good times and bad.

Lord, empower me to trust You when it's hard to remember that You are near. And help me to live thankfully when times are good. Amen.

*"Even now I have one who speaks for me in heaven;
the one who is on my side is high above."*

Job 16:19 ncv

*The Lord looks down from heaven on all mankind to see if there
are any who understand, any who seek God.*

Psalm 14:2 niv

Each of us is precious in the Lord's sight, and He knows our individual stories by heart.
We are His treasures, and He has set aside a special place for us.

*Thank You, Lord, that I am one of Your prized possessions. Keep me ever in Your care.
Amen.*

....
....
....
....
....
....
....
....
....
....
....
....
....
....

Day 196
SIN

. . . .

Therefore, dear brothers and sisters, you have no obligation to do what your sinful nature urges you to do. For if you live by its dictates, you will die. But if through the power of the Spirit you put to death the deeds of your sinful nature, you will live.

ROMANS 8:12–13 NLT

If we confess our sins, he is faithful and just to forgive us our sins, and to cleanse us from all unrighteousness.

1 JOHN 1:9 KJV

Ironically, blood is something that causes a stain that is hard to remove from clothes. But the blood of Jesus eradicates all the dirt on human hearts, removing every stain of sin. No matter how often we fail, we can return, and a simple confession will wash away our sin.

Thank You, Lord, for the cleansing power of Your blood. Amen.

. . . .

. . . .

. . . .

. . . .

. . . .

. . . .

. . . .

. . . .

. . . .

. . . .

If you plan to do evil, you will be lost; if you plan to do good,
you will receive unfailing love and faithfulness.

PROVERBS 14:22 NLT

"For I know the plans I have for you," declares the LORD, "plans to prosper you
and not to harm you, plans to give you hope and a future."

JEREMIAH 29:11 NIV

Looking at our aims or desires for life can give us a picture of what is most important to us individually. As we think of what the coming years will bring, we must remember that the things of earth are temporary. We need to make our plans with eternity in mind. Think beyond long term.

L ord, with You I can have a future full of hope and promise. May my plans be focused on You. Amen.

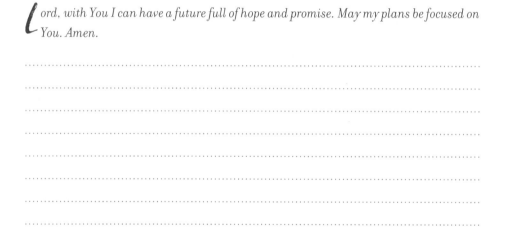

Day 198

HEALTH

....

*But they that wait upon the L*ORD *shall renew their strength; they shall mount up with wings as eagles; they shall run, and not be weary; and they shall walk, and not faint.*

ISAIAH 40:31 KJV

And he said unto me, My grace is sufficient for thee: for my strength is made perfect in weakness. Most gladly therefore will I rather glory in my infirmities, that the power of Christ may rest upon me.

2 CORINTHIANS 12:9 KJV

God wants us to prosper and He loves for us to be in good health, even as our souls prosper. If we really think about that, we have to conclude that the health of our soul is even more important than our physical health. Spend some time today giving your soul a workout.

*L*ord, sometimes I pay more attention to the outside than the inside. Today I draw near to You. Make me healthy—from the inside out. Amen.

....

....

....

....

....

....

....

....

....

So I say, walk by the Spirit, and you will not gratify the desires of the flesh.

GALATIANS 5:16 NIV

As the deer pants for streams of water, so my soul pants for you, my God.
My soul thirsts for God, for the living God. When can I go and meet with God?

PSALM 42:1–2 NIV

If we were completely honest with ourselves, we'd have to admit that our earthly longings usually supersede our longing for God. Ask God to give you His perspective on longing. He knows what it means to long for someone, after all. His longing for you was so great that He gave His only Son on the cross to be near you.

Father, my earthly longings usually get in the way of my spiritual ones. Reignite my longing for You. Amen.

Day 200
GUILT

Keep a clear conscience before God so that when people throw mud at you,
none of it will stick. They'll end up realizing that they're the ones who need a bath.

1 Peter 3:16 msg

"If my people, who are called by my name, will humble themselves and pray
and seek my face and turn from their wicked ways, then I will hear from heaven,
and I will forgive their sin and will heal their land."

2 Chronicles 7:14 niv

When we accept Christ as our Lord and Savior, His life becomes ours. We are no longer slaves to sin, but we own His righteousness. So we don't have to go around thinking that we're scum.

Father God, I praise You for Your forgiveness and healing. Thank You that I am called by Your name. Amen.

....

....

....

....

....

....

....

....

....

....

"Take heed that you do not do your charitable deeds before men, to be seen by them. Otherwise you have no reward from your Father in heaven."

MATTHEW 6:1 NKJV

Recognition comes from God, not legalistic critics.

ROMANS 2:29 MSG

Often we feel as though our good acts are missed. What we need to remember is that none of our actions go unnoticed by God. He sees our every move, and He applauds us when we do good works.

Father, often I feel as though my good behavior is ignored or forgotten. Forgive me for being prideful, and help me to know that You see me at both my best and worst, and love me all the time. Amen.

Day 202
FEAR

....

So that we may boldly say, The Lord is my helper,
and I will not fear what man shall do unto me.

HEBREWS 13:6 KJV

The Spirit you received does not make you slaves, so that you live in fear again; rather,
the Spirit you received brought about your adoption to sonship. And by him we cry,
"Abba, Father."

ROMANS 8:15 NIV

Do you struggle with fear? Do you feel it binding you with its invisible chains? Today, acknowledge your fears to the Lord. He will break your chains and set you free.

Lord, thank You that You are the great chain breaker! I don't have to live in fear. I am Your child, and You are my heavenly Father. Amen.

*So also you, since you are zealous of spiritual gifts,
seek to abound for the edification of the church.*

1 Corinthians 14:12 nasb

*When they found Him, they said to Him, "Everyone is looking for You."
But He said to them, "Let us go into the next towns, that I may preach
there also, because for this purpose I have come forth."*

Mark 1:37–38 nkjv

God designed us for a special purpose. Using our gifts is what we're called to do. When we step into a situation He didn't design for us, we're being disobedient. Filling a position just because there is an opening is never a good idea. We need to find our gifts and use them for God's glory.

Lord, point me on the path You would have me follow. Keep me from being distracted. Amen.

....
....
....
....
....
....
....
....
....
....

Day 204
GRACE

....

*That is the way we should live, because God's grace that can save everyone has
come. It teaches us not to live against God nor to do the evil things the world
wants to do. Instead, that grace teaches us to live in the present age
in a wise and right way and in a way that shows we serve God.*

TITUS 2:11–12 NCV

For by grace are ye saved through faith; and that not of yourselves: it is the gift of God.

EPHESIANS 2:8 KJV

Before we come to know Jesus, our hearts are as cold and dead as winter, full of sin. We
may do many good deeds. But no amount of good can bring a new creation to an unsaved
soul. Only the grace of God has that kind of power.

*God, make a new creation in me. Save me that I might have an abundant life here on
earth and eternal life in heaven. Thank You for grace! Amen.*

....

....

....

....

....

....

....

....

....

....

*"But blessed are those who trust in the Lord
and have made the Lord their hope and confidence."*

JEREMIAH 17:7 NLT

For the Lord will be your confidence, and will keep your foot from being caught.

PROVERBS 3:26 NKJV

Sometimes we wish for more confidence. The next time you need a confidence boost, instead of worrying or trying to muster it up on your own, seek God. Remember that in your weakness, God shows up to be your strength. He will be your confidence.

God, be my confidence when this world brings situations in which I feel insecure or inadequate. Thank You. Amen.

Day 206
APPEARANCE

*On the contrary, we speak as those approved by God to be entrusted with the gospel.
We are not trying to please people but God, who tests our hearts.*

1 THESSALONIANS 2:4 NIV

*Do ye look on things after the outward appearance? If any man trust to himself that he is
Christ's, let him of himself think this again, that, as he is Christ's, even so are we Christ's.*

2 CORINTHIANS 10:7 KJV

It is impossible to please both God and man. We must make a choice. Man looks
at the outward appearance, but God looks at the heart. Align your heart with His.
Receive God's unconditional love and enjoy the freedom to be yourself before Him.

Dear Lord, help me transition from a people pleaser to a God pleaser. Amen.

"But an hour is coming, and now is, when the true worshipers will worship the Father in spirit and truth; for such people the Father seeks to be His worshipers."

JOHN 4:23 NASB

Then the cloud covered the tabernacle of meeting,
and the glory of the LORD filled the tabernacle.

EXODUS 40:34 NKJV

God wants us to enter worship with a heart prepared to meet Him. He longs for us to come in the frame of mind where we're not just singing about Him, we're truly worshiping Him with every fiber of our being. He wants wholehearted participants, not spectators.

Lord, I don't want to go through the motions of worship. Today I offer myself to You, not as a spectator, but as a participant in Your holy presence. Amen.

....
....
....
....
....
....
....
....
....
....
....

Day 208
CONTENTMENT

. . . .

For the despondent, every day brings trouble; for the happy heart, life is a continual feast.

PROVERBS 15:15 NLT

*"If they obey and serve him, they will spend the rest of their days
in prosperity and their years in contentment."*

JOB 36:11 NIV

Even the strongest Christian can struggle with discontentment. We're conditioned by the world to want more. Instead of focusing on all the things you don't have, spend some time praising God for the things you do have. Offer the Lord any discontentment, and watch Him give you a contented heart.

Lord, I confess that I'm not always content. Take my discontentment and replace it with genuine peace. Amen.

*Thou hast turned for me my mourning into dancing: thou hast put off my sackcloth,
and girded me with gladness; to the end that my glory may sing praise to thee,
and not be silent. O Lord my God, I will give thanks unto thee for ever.*

PSALM 30:11–12 KJV

*Not that we are competent in ourselves to claim anything for ourselves,
but our competence comes from God.*

2 CORINTHIANS 3:5 NIV

In times of trouble or weakness, when circumstances seem beyond our control, we pray. But when life is moving along smoothly and we have a handle on life, it is easy to forget who God is and who we are. Scripture teaches us that everything comes from God, even our achievements. Acknowledge the giver behind every good thing you have received.

Heavenly Father, I have been blind to the goodness that dwells in You. Thank You for all Your gifts to me. Amen.

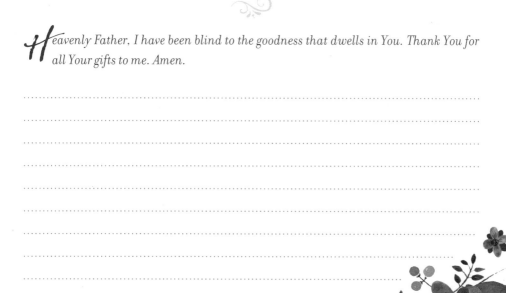

Day 210
HOPE

....

Why, my soul, are you downcast? Why so disturbed within me?
Put your hope in God, for I will yet praise him, my Savior and my God.

PSALM 42:11 NIV

For God alone, O my soul, wait in silence, for my hope is from him.

PSALM 62:5 ESV

Hope is like a little green shoot poking up through hard, cracked ground. When you're depressed, do what David and Jeremiah did—pour out your heart to God. Seek help from a trusted friend or godly counselor. Look for hope. It's all around you, and it's yours for the taking.

Father, even when I am depressed, You are still God. Help me to find a ray of hope in the midst of dark circumstances. Amen.

The LORD is near to the brokenhearted and saves those who are crushed in spirit.

PSALM 34:18 NASB

God is our refuge and strength, an ever-present help in trouble. Therefore we will not fear, though the earth give way and the mountains fall into the heart of the sea.

PSALM 46:1–2 NIV

If you are in a place of sadness, trust in this: there will come a day, an hour, a moment when God will transform gloom into joy. Your feet will be planted on a mountain, where once you fought to climb out of a valley. Suffering is but for a time, and God's mercies are new every day.

Father, when You find me in the pit, put a new song of praise in my heart that I might live again a life of abundance and joy. Amen.

....
....
....
....
....
....
....
....
....
....
....
....
....
....

Day 212
GOD'S LOVE

. . . .

But God demonstrates his own love for us in this:
While we were still sinners, Christ died for us.

ROMANS 5:8 NIV

"For the mountains may depart and the hills be removed, but my steadfast love
shall not depart from you, and my covenant of peace shall no
t be removed," says the LORD, who has compassion on you.

ISAIAH 54:10 ESV

Mountains will move before God's love will leave us. In the sacrifice of Christ on the cross, He demonstrated His amazing love for us. Regardless of what we have done or will do, God's love is set upon us. By faith, we have only to believe what Jesus has done for us.

*F*ather, I thank You for Your unmovable love. Amen.

. . . .
. . . .
. . . .
. . . .
. . . .
. . . .
. . . .
. . . .
. . . .
. . . .
. . . .

* *

*And God shall wipe away all tears from their eyes; and there shall be no more death,
neither sorrow, nor crying, neither shall there be any more pain:
for the former things are passed away.*

REVELATION 21:4 KJV

*My flesh and my heart faileth: but God is the strength of my heart,
and my portion for ever.*

PSALM 73:26 KJV

There are very few things that can be counted on to last forever. Souls are eternal; they remain even when our earthly bodies decay. We need to see beyond the physical by focusing on the spiritual. There is life beyond what we are experiencing in this moment.

Dear Lord, help us keep an eternal focus when we struggle with the physical limitations of our bodies here on earth. Amen.

. . . .
. . . .
. . . .
. . . .
. . . .
. . . .
. . . .
. . . .
. . . .
. . . .

Day 214
FAMILY

Wives, submit to your own husbands, as to the Lord. For the husband is head of the wife, as also Christ is head of the church; and He is the Savior of the body. Therefore, just as the church is subject to Christ, so let the wives be to their own husbands in everything. Husbands, love your wives, just as Christ also loved the church and gave Himself for her.

EPHESIANS 5:22–25 NKJV

Consequently, you are no longer foreigners and strangers, but fellow citizens with God's people and also members of his household.

EPHESIANS 2:19 NIV

How wonderful to know God has made you part of His household! You're not an outcast. You're priceless to Him. He loves you as a child of God more deeply than you can fathom.

Father, thank You for inviting me into Your wonderful family. I praise You for loving me as if I were an only child. Amen.

. . . .

Then he passed in front of Moses and called out, "I am the Lᴏʀᴅ God. I am merciful and very patient with my people. I show great love, and I can be trusted."

Exodus 34:6 ᴄᴇᴠ

The Lᴏʀᴅ is merciful! He is kind and patient, and his love never fails.

Psalm 103:8 ᴄᴇᴠ

We humans are impatient and want what we want right now. But our Father in heaven knows better. He has created a world that unfolds according to His timetable. Wait for God to reveal His perfect plan. He's in control.

D ear Lord, You know my heart's desires. Help me to wait upon Your answer for my life. Amen.

. . . .
. . . .
. . . .
. . . .
. . . .
. . . .
. . . .
. . . .
. . . .
. . . .
. . . .
. . . .
. . . .
. . . .

Day 216
SHARING THE GOSPEL

Therefore do not be ashamed of the testimony about our Lord.

2 TIMOTHY 1:8 ESV

Jesus said, "I tell you the truth, all those who have left houses, brothers, sisters, mother, father, children, or farms for me and for the Good News will get more than they left."

MARK 10:29–30 NCV

The lives of those people who are touched by the love of Christ are like guiding lights to others who have yet to find Christ. They can provide guidance and help, and they shine forth as bright examples of how good life can be.

Father, please make me a light for my world. Let me shine forth with Your goodness, care, and love. Amen.

For the love of money is a root of all kinds of evil. Some people, eager for money, have wandered from the faith and pierced themselves with many griefs.

1 TIMOTHY 6:10 NIV

"No one can serve two masters. Either you will hate the one and love the other, or you will be devoted to the one and despise the other. You cannot serve both God and money."

MATTHEW 6:24 NIV

As you feel yourself start to worry about money, stop and change your focus from wealth to God. Thank Him for what He has provided for you and then humbly ask Him to give you wisdom about your financial situation.

Dear God, help me remember that I can absolutely trust You to provide for me and to sustain me. Amen.

Day 218
FORGIVENESS

"Take heed to yourselves. If your brother sins against you, rebuke him; and if he repents, forgive him. And if he sins against you seven times in a day, and seven times in a day returns to you, saying, 'I repent,' you shall forgive him."

LUKE 17:3–4 NKJV

Bear with each other and forgive one another if any of you has a grievance against someone. Forgive as the Lord forgave you.

COLOSSIANS 3:13 NIV

People—even loved ones—sometimes say and do hurtful things. Instead of holding a grudge against these people, Jesus has another answer: hand the hurt over to Him and forgive. Forgiveness is a process that is successful only with God's help. After all, He's the perfect example of forgiveness, forgiving us again and again. . .and again.

Jesus, give me strength to let go of bad feelings and forgive. Amen.

Laughter can conceal a heavy heart, but when the laughter ends, the grief remains.
PROVERBS 14:13 NLT

A cheerful disposition is good for your health; gloom and doom leave you bone-tired.
PROVERBS 17:22 MSG

It's a scientifically proven fact that laughter lowers blood pressure and strengthens the immune system. In short, laughter is good medicine. Imagine the effect we could have on our world today if our countenances reflected the joy of the Lord. Maybe it's time we looked for something to laugh about.

ord, help me find happiness in this day. Let me laugh and give praises to the King. Amen.

Day 220
TRUST

. . . .

Many are the woes of the wicked,
but the LORD's unfailing love surrounds the one who trusts in him.

PSALM 32.10 NIV

Trust in the LORD with all thine heart; and lean not unto thine own understanding.
In all thy ways acknowledge him, and he shall direct thy paths.

PROVERBS 3:5–6 KJV

Try trusting the Lord with all your heart. Not just a little piece of your heart, but all of it. Remember, it's really pretty simple: you either trust Him or you don't.

*D*ear Lord, I trust You with all my heart and all my being. I acknowledge You as Lord of my life. Amen.

Anger is cruel, and wrath is like a flood, but jealousy is even more dangerous.

PROVERBS 27:4 NLT

*A peaceful heart leads to a healthy body;
jealousy is like cancer in the bones.*

PROVERBS 14:30 NLT

When we compare ourselves to others we become jealous, and this jealousy has a way of growing like cancer—quickly and out of control. It can wreak havoc with our inner lives because we are never satisfied, never at peace. For true satisfaction, we must look to God and God alone.

Heavenly Father, guard my heart against comparing myself to others. Help me to be at peace. Amen.

Day 222
FALSE TEACHING

Now if Christ is preached that He has been raised from the dead,
how do some among you say that there is no resurrection of the dead?

1 Corinthians 15:12 nkjv

"Then if anyone tells you, 'Look, here is the Messiah,' or 'There he is,' don't believe it.
For false messiahs and false prophets will rise up and perform signs and wonders
so as to deceive, if possible, even God's chosen ones. Watch out!
I have warned you about this ahead of time!"

Mark 13:21–23 nlt

Only God can give us the help and support we need to deal with the regular pressures of life. There is no other way, for it is only with God that all things are possible.

There is no answer apart from You, almighty God! In every situation, both good and bad,
You are my strength and my hope. Amen.

....
....
....
....
....
....
....
....
....
....
....

*You will show me the way of life, granting me the joy of your presence
and the pleasures of living with you forever.*

PSALM 16:11 NLT

*You make known to me the path of life; you will fill me with joy in your presence,
with eternal pleasures at your right hand.*

PSALM 16:11 NIV

Our Creator God is a joy giver, and He pours it out when you need it most. At your
very lowest point, He's there, ready to fill you with that bubbling-over kind of joy.
And how wonderful to know that in His right hand there is happiness forever.

*O Lord, I need joy today. Thank You for the reminder that You are a joy giver and that
You want me to be happy. Pour out Your joy, Father! Amen.*

Day 224
WORRY

"And you? Go about your business without fretting or worrying. Relax. When it's all over, you will be on your feet to receive your reward."

DANIEL 12:13 MSG

"So don't worry about tomorrow, for tomorrow will bring its own worries. Today's trouble is enough for today."

MATTHEW 6:34 NLT

If we're honest with ourselves, we admit we sometimes hold on to our worries, thinking that keeping them close somehow keeps us in control of the situation. In reality, most of our worries concern things completely out of our hands. Instead, Jesus offers us freedom from our chains of worry.

Jesus, You know the toll worries take on my heart and mind. Help me to place my concerns in Your capable hands so that I can be free to praise You. Amen.

Then He said to them, "Beware, and be on your guard against every form of greed; for not even when one has an abundance does his life consist of his possessions."

Luke 12:15 NASB

"You shall not covet your neighbor's house; you shall not covet your neighbor's wife, nor his male servant, nor his female servant, nor his ox, nor his donkey, nor anything that is your neighbor's."

Exodus 20:17 NKJV

To covet means to feel unreasonable desire for something that belongs to another. The Lord knows we have wishes and dreams, but He wants us to have the right perspective on them and not let them control our lives. Wish for anything you want; covet nothing.

Lord, help me to keep my desires under control. Help me live in contentment with the many things You've blessed me with. Amen.

Day 226
PEACE

. . . .

In peace I will lie down and sleep, for you alone, O Lord, will keep me safe.

PSALM 4:8 NLT

The Lord gives perfect peace to those whose faith is firm.

ISAIAH 26:3 CEV

In every age, in every place, there are people who live by the rule of violence. How much better it is to live a life of peace and love.

Rule in my heart with peace and love, Lord. Amen.

Then I heard a voice from heaven, saying, "Write these words:
'From now on those who are dead who died belonging to the Lord will be happy.'"

REVELATION 14:13 NLV

"For truly, I say to you, whoever gives you a cup of water to drink
because you belong to Christ will by no means lose his reward."

MARK 9:41 ESV

When the Lord said He has engraved us on the palms of His hands, He was telling us that He remembers us. All day every day, He remembers us. We are of utmost importance to Him. We cannot be forgotten.

Father, thank You that through Christ You have brought me to Yourself, You reign over my life, and You always remember me. Amen.

Day 228
OBEDIENCE

· ·

Blessed are all who fear the Lord, who walk in obedience to him.

PSALM 128:1 NIV

But if we walk in the light as He is in the light, we have fellowship with one another, and the blood of Jesus Christ His Son cleanses us from all sin.

1 JOHN 1:7 NKJV

How do we remain in the light? We ask the Holy Spirit to guide us, and when we get an uneasy feeling regarding a choice, we pay attention to it. It may be hard to say no, but the payoff for obedience will be great.

Father of light, help me to be sensitive to Your Holy Spirit. Shine Your light into my life. Amen.

O Lord, who shall sojourn in your tent? Who shall dwell on your holy hill?
He who walks blamelessly and does what is right and speaks truth in his heart.

PSALM 15:1–2 ESV

The Lord is near to all who call on him, to all who call on him in truth.

PSALM 145:18 ESV

Honesty is a valuable virtue. We have the power to change lives when we speak the truth. If we tell people fables, we lose credibility and weaken our power to help them.

Father, let me be honest and open so that I might have the opportunity to make a difference in lives. Amen.

· ·

Mockers are proud and haughty; they act with boundless arrogance.

PROVERBS 21:24 NLT

Pride ends in humiliation, while humility brings honor.

PROVERBS 29:23 NLT

Remembering that everything is a gift from God—even our accomplishments—is hard. If we're not careful, we can begin to think we've brought about those things ourselves. Nothing could be further from the truth. Every detail of our lives is orchestrated by God.

*R*emind me daily, Father, that every good and perfect gift comes not from my hard work, but from You. Amen.

Others have praised God for what he has done, so join with them.

Job 36:24 cev

Through Jesus, therefore, let us continually offer to God a sacrifice of praise—the fruit of lips that openly profess his name.

Hebrews 13:15 niv

Jesus was willing to live among us, suffer, and die on the cross for us. How do we respond? With a sacrifice of praise. God desires to hear us praise Jesus. God is pleased with our faith in Jesus and our sacrifice of praise.

Father, I praise You for clothing me in the righteousness of Christ. May my life reflect His transforming grace. Amen.

Day 232
FEAR

The fear of man bringeth a snare: but whoso putteth his trust in the LORD shall be safe.

PROVERBS 29:25 KJV

For I, the LORD your God, hold your right hand; it is I who say to you, "Fear not, I am the one who helps you."

ISAIAH 41:13 ESV

God holds your hand. He protects you. He is with you in your darkest moments. With the clasp of His hand comes courage for any situation. He tells you not to fear, for He is your ever-present help in times of trouble.

A lmighty God, forgive me for the times I let fear reign in my life. Grant me the courage that comes from knowing You are my helper. Amen.

REFLECTING CHRIST

*Let your light so shine before men, that they may see your good works,
and glorify your Father which is in heaven.*

MATTHEW 5:16 KJV

*For if anyone is a hearer of the word and not a doer, he is like a man who looks
intently at his natural face in a mirror. For he looks at himself
and goes away and at once forgets what he was like.*

JAMES 1:23–24 ESV

Loving the unlovable, giving to the needy, forgiving the unforgivable, being honest, and striving to be Christlike are all perfect ways to share the light of Jesus. Let your life be a beacon of light and hope to all you meet.

Dear Lord, thank You for bringing light to my darkness. Help me to spread the light of Jesus to those who don't know You. Amen.

Day 234
FEARING GOD

Saying with a loud voice, Fear God, and give glory to him; for the hour of his judgment is come: and worship him that made heaven, and earth, and the sea, and the fountains of waters.

REVELATION 14:7 KJV

Only fear the LORD, and serve him in truth with all your heart: for consider how great things he hath done for you.

1 SAMUEL 12:24 KJV

We stand in awe before God, wisely cautious in the face of His power, and yet we long to know Him, to be united with Him. The wise pursue Him with all their hearts, while the foolish ignore Him or reject Him through their fear.

O Lord, help me to know fear in a positive way. Allow me to feel healthy fear, but never let that fear separate me from You. Amen.

From his abundance we have all received one gracious blessing after another.
For the law was given through Moses, but God's unfailing
love and faithfulness came through Jesus Christ.

JOHN 1:16–17 NLT

LORD, you alone are my inheritance, my cup of blessing. You guard all that is mine.

PSALM 16:5 NLT

Once we have a relationship with God the Father through Jesus Christ, we are in line for a multitude of blessings. Why do we not recognize all our blessings? Because it's human nature to zero in on what's wrong and miss what's very right. We need to open our arms and become thankful recipients for all He's given.

ord, You have given me so much, and I am thankful. Let me give thanks for Your gifts. Amen.

Day 236
SIN

But now that you have been set free from sin and have become slaves of God, the fruit you get leads to sanctification and its end, eternal life. For the wages of sin is death, but the free gift of God is eternal life in Christ Jesus our Lord.

ROMANS 6:22–23 ESV

"Yet they say to each other, 'Don't come too close or you will defile me! I am holier than you!' These people are a stench in my nostrils, an acrid smell that never goes away."

ISAIAH 65:5 NLT

No good end can come from a life of sin. Ultimately, we must answer for our actions before God. If we do not repent of our misdeeds, we find ourselves hopelessly separated from God. But with God's help, we will never be ensnared.

Forgive my sins, almighty God, and help me to live the life You desire—free from sin and devoted to You. Amen.

Daniel said, "I saw in my vision by night, and behold, the four winds of heaven were stirring up the great sea (the nations)."

DANIEL 7:2 AMP

"Step out of the traffic! Take a long, loving look at me, your High God, above politics, above everything."

PSALM 46:10 MSG

Voting is our duty and privilege as citizens. But whether we line up with the conservative or liberal side of politics, we must not trust in government—or any politician—to save us. Jesus Christ is the only Savior. And He never breaks any of His promises.

Lord, thank You that You promise to take care of us. Help us not to put too much trust in men or agencies. Amen.

Day 238
COMFORT

· ·

Give me a sign of your goodness, that my enemies may see it
and be put to shame, for you, LORD, have helped me and comforted me.

PSALM 86:17 NIV

All praise to God, the Father of our Lord Jesus Christ. God is our merciful Father and the
source of all comfort. He comforts us in all our troubles so that we can comfort others.
When they are troubled, we will be able to give them the same comfort God has given us.

2 CORINTHIANS 1:3–4 NLT

God is the greatest source of comfort the human spirit will ever encounter. As God
comforts us, we can comfort others. Is there someone in your life who could use some
comfort? Offer it in any small way that you are able.

*M*erciful Father, comfort me in my times of need and show me those that I might
comfort. Amen.

· ·

· ·

· ·

· ·

· ·

· ·

· ·

· ·

· ·

· ·

*Let all bitterness, and wrath, and anger, and clamour, and evil speaking,
be put away from you, with all malice.*

Ephesians 4:31 KJV

*Don't make friends with quick-tempered people or spend time with those who have
bad tempers. If you do, you will be like them. Then you will be in real danger.*

Proverbs 22:24–25 NCV

Following the Golden Rule—doing unto others as you would have them do unto you—and loving others as you love yourself is tough to do when you're arguing. But just how important is it to prove your point in the grand scheme of things?

Lord, show me what to say and what not to say to avoid strife. Give me Your heart toward others. Amen.

....
....
....
....
....
....
....
....
....
....
....
....

Day 240
ENCOURAGEMENT

*I am acting with great boldness toward you; I have great pride in you;
I am filled with comfort. In all our affliction, I am overflowing with joy.*

2 CORINTHIANS 7:4 ESV

*So if there is any encouragement in Christ, any comfort from love, any participation in
the Spirit, any affection and sympathy, complete my joy by being of the same
mind, having the same love, being in full accord and of one mind.*

PHILIPPIANS 2:1 ESV

Let's encourage one another to take steps of faith—to get out of our comfortable boats. Through our own example, we can inspire others to desire to follow Jesus. As we experience life together, let's spur one another on toward love and good deeds!

Dear Lord, help me look for ways to encourage others in their Christian walk. May my words and life inspire them to follow Jesus. Amen.

Be still before the Lord and wait patiently for him.

PSALM 37:7 NIV

Lord, I wait for you; you will answer, Lord my God.

PSALM 38:15 NIV

Waiting on God is hard. But God's Word tells us to wait patiently—with peace. Rather than sighing with impatience, try praying, reading scripture, and making your waiting time productive and meaningful. Wait patiently and with confidence. God will come through.

Heavenly Father, when the waiting seems unbearable, remind me that Your timing is always perfect. Amen.

Day 242
ETERNITY

· ·

" 'I will do it for anyone who carries out my plans to the end.
I will give that person authority over the nations.' "

REVELATION 2:26 NIrv

But as it is written, Eye hath not seen, nor ear heard, neither have entered into
the heart of man, the things which God hath prepared for them that love him.

1 CORINTHIANS 2:9 KJV

God doesn't want any of us to suffer, especially eternally. In His infinite love, God provided us with another way. He gave us a new Tree of Life, His Son, Jesus Christ.

Thank You, O Lord, for giving me the chance to have eternal life. Through Your love, I have come to know Your glory. Amen.

· ·

· ·

· ·

· ·

· ·

· ·

· ·

· ·

· ·

· ·

· ·

· ·

GOD'S PROVISION

*And Isaac spake unto Abraham his father, and said, My father: and he said, Here am I,
my son. And he said, Behold the fire and the wood: but where is the lamb for a
burnt offering? And Abraham said, My son, God will provide himself a
lamb for a burnt offering: so they went both of them together.*

GENESIS 22:7–8 KJV

*Hitherto have ye asked nothing in my name:
ask, and ye shall receive, that your joy may be full.*

JOHN 16:24 KJV

Often we ask God for more than our daily needs. We look into the future, and with
fearful hearts we plead with God concerning our needs. We don't give God the chance
to show us that He will provide day by day. In the coming days, try to rely on God for
daily provision without asking for more.

*God, give me this day my daily bread. Let me trust You for this day, believing You are a
God who knows my needs. Amen.*

Day 244
SALVATION

Therefore, my beloved, as you have always obeyed, not as in my presence only,
but now much more in my absence, work out your own salvation with fear and
trembling, for it is God who works in you both to will and to do for His good pleasure.

PHILIPPIANS 2:12–13 NKJV

Like newborn babies, crave pure spiritual milk, so that by it you may grow up
in your salvation, now that you have tasted that the Lord is good.

1 PETER 2:2–3 NIV

Our salvation is a well. In it is not only our eternal life, but also our abundant life while we live on earth. Christ is the living water, continually refreshing and nourishing us, giving life to our bodies and souls. Daily we need to go to the well of our salvation, remembering our need for Jesus and drawing out the living with joy.

Lord, thank You for saving me. Cause me to remember that my life is hidden in Yours.
Amen.

FOLLOWING JESUS

Then Jesus spoke to them again, saying, "I am the light of the world. He who follows Me shall not walk in darkness, but have the light of life."

And now, Israel, what does the LORD your God ask of you but to fear the LORD your God, to walk in obedience to him, to love him, to serve the LORD your God with all your heart and with all your soul, and to observe the LORD's commands and decrees that I am giving you today for your own good?

The pursuit of God is one of the few life choices we can make that has no strings attached. We give very little and receive so much.

Lord, the gift of knowing You is given freely. When life distracts me, help me to seek You with all my heart. Amen.

....

My son, keep your father's command, and do not forsake the law of your mother.

PROVERBS 6:20 NKJV

So in Christ Jesus you are all children of God through faith.

GALATIANS 3:26 NIV

Whether your childhood reflected love or abandonment, there is good news! As a Christian, you are a child of the King of kings, the Lord of lords, the sovereign God. You are not just God's friend or distant relative. You are His child!

Thank You, Father, for adopting me through Christ. Teach me to live as a reflection of my Father's love. Amen.

Day 247
REPENTANCE

. . . .

*"Repent, then, and turn to God, so that your sins may be wiped out,
that times of refreshing may come from the Lord."*

ACTS 3:19 NIV

*And he said, "Who told you that you were naked? Have you eaten from the tree that
I commanded you not to eat from?" The man said, "The woman you put her
with me—she gave me some fruit from the tree, and I ate it."*

GENESIS 3:11–12 NIV

If you long to be like Christ, determine today not to play the "blame game" anymore.
When confronted with sin, ask God for His mercy and accept His forgiveness.

*Lord, give me the strength of character to admit when I'm wrong and turn from my sin.
Amen.*

Day 248
LONELINESS

The time will come and is already here when all of you will be scattered.
Each of you will go back home and leave me by myself. But the Father
will be with me, and I won't be alone.

JOHN 16:32 CEV

For I am persuaded, that neither death, nor life, nor angels, nor principalities,
nor powers, nor things present, nor things to come, nor height, nor depth,
nor any other creature, shall be able to separate us from
the love of God, which is in Christ Jesus our Lord.

ROMANS 8:38–39 KJV

Everyone experiences loneliness sometimes. God promises that He will never leave you nor forsake you. You can have full confidence in knowing that with God's love, you'll never, ever be alone.

Dear God, according to Your Word, if I dwell in love, I dwell with You. Remind me that nothing can separate me from You, not even feelings of loneliness. Amen.

· ·

Blessed is the man that endureth temptation: for when he is tried, he shall receive the crown of life, which the Lord hath promised to them that love him.

JAMES 1.12 KJV

Because thou hast kept the word of my patience, I also will keep thee from the hour of temptation, which shall come upon all the world, to try them that dwell upon the earth.

REVELATION 3:10 KJV

Evil abounds in our fallen world, and there are temptations around every corner. The devil never takes a day off. Be wary. We need to turn away from the lure of evil and place our lives in the center of God's will.

Lord, help me to put on Your armor and obey Your Word so that ultimate victory will be Yours. Amen.

· ·

Day 250
SPIRITUAL REFRESHMENT

Let's do our best to know the LORD. His coming is as certain as the morning sun; he will refresh us like rain renewing the earth in the springtime.

HOSEA 6.3 CEV

Take My yoke upon you and learn from Me [following Me as My disciple], for I am gentle and humble in heart, and you will find rest (renewal, blessed quiet) for your souls

MATTHEW 11:29 AMP

Reading the Bible, going to church, fellowshipping with other believers, praying; these and many other activities draw us close to God and therefore energize our spiritual lives.

Lord, draw me close to You. I need a spiritual boost today. Amen.

The Lᴏʀᴅ is constantly watching everyone,
and he gives strength to those who faithfully obey him.

2 Cʜʀᴏɴɪᴄʟᴇs 16.9 ᴄᴇᴠ

He gives strength to the weary and increases the power of the weak.

Isᴀɪᴀʜ 40:29 ɴɪᴠ

A strong spiritual core will help ensure that you remain stable and secure in a changing world, that you are able to keep from falling. As you exercise your physical body, also make a commitment to regularly exercise your spiritual core as well.

ather, help me to return again and again to the core foundations of my spiritual health. Amen.

....
....
....
....
....
....
....
....
....
....
....
....
....

Day 252
EVIL

....

Turn your back on evil, work for the good and don't quit. God loves this kind of thing.
PSALM 37:27–28 MSG

Do not be overcome by evil, but overcome evil with good.
ROMANS 12:21 NASB

You are placed at this point in history for a reason. God has a job—a specific purpose—for you. You are a believer in Jesus Christ in a world that is increasingly hostile to Him in order that you might shine the light of His love.

Lord, I know You want me to overcome evil with good. Give me the courage to do just that. Amen.

....

....

....

....

....

....

....

....

....

....

....

Lord, see how my enemies persecute me!
Have mercy and lift me up from the gates of death.

PSALM 9:13 NIV

Persecuted, but not forsaken; cast down, but not destroyed.

2 CORINTHIANS 4:9 KJV

God promises that even though we may be persecuted at times, He will never forsake us. That means He's right there, walking us through the pain. And even when we're cast down, we will never be destroyed. If we stick close to Jesus, we are buoyed by His faithfulness.

Father, when I go through seasons of persecution, I know You will walk with me. Amen!

Day 254
GOD'S GLORY

*Thine, O Lord is the greatness, and the power, and the glory, and the victory,
and the majesty: for all that is in the heaven and in the earth is thine.*

1 Chronicles 29:11 kjv

*So shall they fear the name of the Lord from the west, and His glory from the rising
of the sun; when the enemy comes in like a flood, the Spirit
of the Lord will lift up a standard against him.*

Isaiah 59:19 nkjv

Knowing the power of the name and glory of the Lord is essential to our Christian lives. His name is above every other name; none has more authority than the One who spoke the world into being. His glory fills the whole earth.

Lord, forgive me for forgetting how powerful You are and that Your glory is displayed throughout the whole earth. Help me remember who my God is. Amen.

"Boast no more so very proudly, do not let arrogance come out of your mouth; for the LORD is a God of knowledge, and with Him actions are weighed."

1 SAMUEL 2:3 NASB

Make the most of every opportunity in these evil days. Don't act thoughtlessly, but understand what the Lord wants you to do.

EPHESIANS 5:16–17 NLT

Are you an actor or a reactor? The Lord longs for us to think before we act—to act on His behalf. To react takes little or no thought, but to live a life that reflects the image of Christ takes lots of work!

God, today I give You my knee-jerking tendencies. Guard my actions. Amen.

Day 256
PERSEVERANCE

Not only so, but we also glory in our sufferings, because we know that suffering produces perseverance; perseverance, character; and character, hope.

ROMANS 5.3–4 NIV

With your help I can advance against a troop; with my God I can scale a wall.

PSALM 18:29 NIV

We often become discouraged when we face a mountain-size task. Tasks like these are best faced one step at a time, chipping away instead of moving the whole mountain at once. With perseverance, and God's help, your goals may be more attainable than you think.

D ear Father, when tasks seem impossible, remind me to seek You. With Your help each step of the way, I will succeed. Amen.

*For I will not trust in my bow, nor will my sword save me. But You have saved us
from our adversaries, and You have put to shame those who hate us.*

PSALM 44:6–7 NASB

*He was oppressed, and he was afflicted, yet he opened not his mouth; like a lamb
that is led to the slaughter, and like a sheep that before its
shearers is silent, so he opened not his mouth.*

ISAIAH 53:7 ESV

Jesus' silence can teach us important lessons. Underneath His silence was an implicit
trust in His Father and His purposes. Christ knew who He was and what He had come
to do. Trust is built in silence, and confidence strengthens in silence.

*Lord Jesus, help me to learn from Your silence. Help me to trust You more so that I don't
feel the need to explain myself. Amen.*

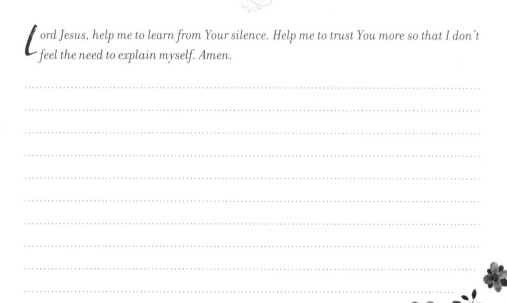

Day 258
AMBITION

*Now listen, you who say, "Today or tomorrow we will go to this or that city,
spend a year there, carry on business and make money." Why, you do not even
know what will happen tomorrow. What is your life? You are a mist that
appears for a little while and then vanishes. Instead, you ought to say,
"If it is the Lord's will, we will live and do this or that."*

JAMES 4:13–15 NIV

*For where you have envy and selfish ambition,
there you find disorder and every evil practice.*

JAMES 3:16 NIV

It is easy to fall into a trap of trying to live up to society's standards. This is sad, because
who we should really be trying to please is God. He has created each of us with special
gifts and talents, and it is His will that we do nothing more than live up to the potential
He created for us.

*Lord, help me to realize my potential. Make me less a person pleaser, and more a God
pleaser. Amen.*

*"May he turn our hearts to him, to walk in obedience to him and keep
the commands, decrees and laws he gave our ancestors."*

1 Kings 8:58 niv

*"Do not add to or subtract from these commands I am giving you.
Just obey the commands of the Lord your God that I am giving you."*

Deuteronomy 4:2 nlt

Following the unknown path that God has prepared leads us to a greater obedience,
obedience that helps us to learn more of Him. This newfound knowledge will ultimately
lead to happiness and contentment.

*Father, guide me on Your path. Help me to learn of You and use what You teach me for
Your glory. Amen.*

Day 260
FOLLOWING JESUS

*And walk in love, as Christ also hath loved us, and hath given himself for us
an offering and a sacrifice to God for a sweetsmelling savour.*

EPHESIANS 5:2 KJV

*For we are his workmanship, created in Christ Jesus unto good works, which God hath
before ordained that we should walk in them.*

EPHESIANS 2:10 KJV

Jesus asked His disciples to follow Him, and He asks us to do the same. It sounds
simple, but following Jesus can be a challenge. Sometimes we become impatient,
not wanting to wait upon the Lord. Or perhaps we aren't diligent to keep in step with
Him. Following Jesus requires staying right on His heels.

Jesus, grant me the desire to follow You. Help me not to run ahead or lag behind. Amen.

Put to death therefore what is earthly in you: sexual immorality, impurity, passion, evil desire, and covetousness, which is idolatry.

COLOSSIANS 3:5 ESV

The idols of the nations are silver and gold, the work of men's hands. They have mouths, but they do not speak; eyes they have, but they do not see; they have ears, but they do not hear; nor is there any breath in their mouths. Those who make them are like them; so is everyone who trusts in them.

PSALM 135:15–18 NKJV

Idols can be made from good things like relationships, families, religion, or work. Anything we love and desire more than Christ becomes an idol. But idols are powerless compared to our God. Spend time in prayer and ask God to reveal any powerless idols you serve.

*G*reat Savior, who died to set me free, please show me the things I love more than You. Amen.

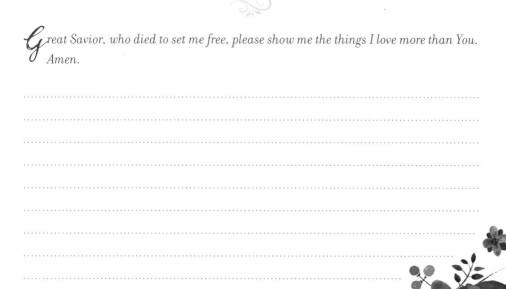

Day 262
HELPING OTHERS

*First, God chose some people to be apostles and prophets and teachers for the church.
But he also chose some to work miracles or heal the sick or help
others or be leaders or speak different kinds of languages.*

1 Corinthians 12:28 cev

*"Give, and it will be given to you. A good measure, pressed down, shaken together and running
over, will be poured into your lap. For with the measure you use, it will be measured to you."*

Luke 6:38 niv

The Bible tells us to help carry each other's loads. There's someone out there who needs
your help. Ask God to show you that person and what you can do to help meet his or
her needs. Giving to others will always bring an abundance of blessings back to you.

ear God, show me ways to help others so I bring glory and honor to Your name. Amen.

Do you not know that your bodies are temples of the Holy Spirit, who is in you,
whom you have received from God? You are not your own; you were bought
at a price. Therefore honor God with your bodies.

1 Corinthians 6:19–20 niv

O Lord, I know that the way of man is not in himself: it is not in man that walketh
to direct his steps. O Lord, correct me, but with judgment;
not in thine anger, lest thou bring me to nothing.

Jeremiah 10:23–24 kjv

Our hearts are wicked, and we can't understand our own feelings and actions.
Thankfully, God has given us the gift of the Holy Spirit to help us on our journey.
If we ask, the Lord is faithful to His Word and He will reveal our motivations to us.

Thank You, Father, that You are the discerner of hearts, that You have given me Your
Holy Spirit to help me. Amen.

Day 264
GOD'S WORD

He who keeps God's Word keeps his soul, but he who is not careful of his ways will die.

PROVERBS 19:16 NLV

"The Spirit gives life; the flesh counts for nothing.
The words I have spoken to you—they are full of the Spirit and life."

JOHN 6:63 NIV

How God works through His Word is a mystery, but He does. When we hear it, meditate on it, pray it, memorize it, and ask for faith to believe it, He comes to us in it and transforms our lives through it.

Thank You, Jesus, the Living Word, who changes my heart and my mind through the power of Your Word. Amen.

*How much more is done by the blood of Christ. He offered himself through the eternal
Spirit as a perfect sacrifice to God. His blood will make our consciences
pure from useless acts so we may serve the living God.*

HEBREWS 9:14 NCV

*"But if serving the LORD seems undesirable to you, then choose for yourselves this day
whom you will serve. . . . But as for me and my household, we will serve the LORD."*

JOSHUA 24:15 NIV

We must choose whom we will serve. The truth is, we all serve something. We may
serve careers, money, appearance, or even relationships. Although we may not admit
it, we become slaves to whatever we choose to serve. Choose to serve the Lord!

*D ear Lord, forgive me for choosing to serve anything other than You. Help me to
faithfully love You. Amen.*

. . . .

. . . .

. . . .

. . . .

. . . .

. . . .

. . . .

. . . .

. . . .

. . . .

. . . .

Day 266
PRIORITIES

"You blind men, which is more important, the offering,
or the altar that sanctifies the offering?"

MATTHEW 23:19 NASB

Before daybreak the next morning, Jesus got up and went out to an isolated place to pray.

MARK 1:35 NLT

Jesus' days were packed with urgency. And yet He never seemed to be in a hurry and always accomplished everything that needed to be done. His secret? Jesus' priorities were clearly in order. He did the important things—like spending time with His Father—first.

Father, order my priorities; help me to put You first and to trust You to help me do the rest. Amen.

ACCEPTANCE

*"Cease striving and know that I am God; I will be exalted among the nations,
I will be exalted in the earth."*

PSALM 46:10 NASB

*Then David got up from the ground. After he had washed, put on lotions and changed
his clothes, he went into the house of the LORD and worshiped. Then he went
to his own house, and at his request they served him food, and he ate.*

2 SAMUEL 12:20 NIV

Acceptance of difficult situations isn't denial, and it isn't acting as if nothing has
happened. It is a quiet surrender, opening ourselves to the Lord's work in our hearts.

*Heavenly Father, help me to accept what You offer me—the good and the bad. Help me
to worship You in my pain. Amen.*

. . . .

Day 268
ENCOURAGEMENT

....

As soon as I pray, you answer me; you encourage me by giving me strength.

PSALM 138:3 NLT

*But do not forget this one thing, dear friends: With the Lord a day is like
a thousand years, and a thousand years are like a day.*

2 PETER 3:8 NIV

If you are feeling discouraged, take a step back and look at the big picture. Ask God to give you some of His perspective. Maintaining a biblical perspective on our circumstances can mean the difference between peace and anxiety, between joy and sorrow.

Father, I admit that I often become discouraged. Please give me a fresh perspective to see life through Your eyes. Amen.

....
....
....
....
....
....
....
....
....
....
....
....

*In a loud voice they were saying: "Worthy is the Lamb, who was slain,
to receive power and wealth and wisdom and strength and honor and glory and praise!"*

REVELATION 5:12 NIV

I can do all things through Christ who strengthens me.

PHILIPPIANS 4:13 NKJV

It's human nature to try to handle things on our own. But the same God who created the heavens and the earth stands ready to work through you. Talk about power! It's above and beyond anything we could ever ask for or think of.

God, today I lean on Your strength. Remind me daily that I can do all things through You. Amen.

Day 270
PROCRASTINATION

Jesus said, "No procrastination. No backward looks. You can't put God's kingdom off till tomorrow. Seize the day."

LUKE 9:62 MSG

Farmers who wait for perfect weather never plant.
If they watch every cloud, they never harvest.

ECCLESIASTES 11:4 NLT

Make a list of the things you've been putting off, then begin today to work through the list. With each item crossed off, you'll find it becomes easier to tackle the next.

Father, I'm avoiding some things in my life. Help me take the first step. Amen.

*I said to myself, "Relax, because the L*ORD *takes care of you."*

PSALM 116:7 NCV

And He said to them, "Come aside by yourselves to a deserted place and rest a while."
For there were many coming and going, and they did not even have time to eat.

MARK 6:31 NKJV

In our hurry-scurry world, a seaside vacation might be nice, but it's not always practical. Short periods of time garnered throughout a week might suffice. The front seat of your car, your bedroom, a park bench. All places where conversation with God can restore your soul.

*D*ear Lord, grant me rest during hectic times. Amen.

Day 272
DREAMS

Night is coming for them, and nightmares, for God takes the side of victims.
Do you think you can mess with the dreams of the poor?
You can't, for God makes their dreams come true.

PSALM 14:5–6 MSG

Those who work their land will have plenty of food,
but the one who chases empty dreams is not wise.

PROVERBS 12:11 NCV

When our dreams are dashed, we have a choice. We can wallow in disappointment and cling to lost dreams, or we can look forward to the bright future that God has promised to every believer. It is a choice, and that choice is always ours.

Lord, even when plans don't go my way, help me to trust in the future that You have planned for me. Amen.

I will declare that your love stands firm forever,
that you have established your faithfulness in heaven itself.

PSALM 89:2 NIV

The LORD has established his throne in heaven, and his kingdom rules over all.

PSALM 103:19 NIV

God gives us glimpses of heaven here on earth so that we might long for such a place from the deepest reaches of our hearts.

Father, when I see the beauty of Your creation, it reminds me of the beauty of heaven that awaits. Thank You for the promise of heaven. Amen.

Day 274
PATIENCE

....

Be completely humble and gentle; be patient, bearing with one another in love.

EPHESIANS 4:2 NIV

Wait on the LORD; be of good courage, and He shall strengthen your heart;
wait, I say, on the LORD!

PSALM 27:14 NKJV

God's patience is without question. Sometimes He finds Himself having to repeat something. When our heavenly Father takes the time to repeat Himself, it must be important. He longs to strengthen your heart. How does He do that? He asks you to wait—and wait again.

Father, sometimes I don't think I can keep up my courage. Today I recommit myself to trusting You with all the things I'm waiting for. Amen.

Those who live according to the flesh have their minds set on what the flesh desires; but those who live in accordance with the Spirit have their minds set on what the Spirit desires.

ROMANS 8:5 NIV

The eyes of all look expectantly to You, and You give them their food in due season. You open Your hand and satisfy the desire of every living thing.

PSALM 145:15–16 NKJV

We can give God every desire of our heart. He can satisfy them. Prayer is the link. As you commune with Him, you will find your desires are either fulfilled or they begin to change to the blessings He wants to give you.

Lord, help me to be open and honest before You with all my yearnings. Enable me to trust You to fulfill or change the desires of my heart. Amen.

Day 276
ANGER

A quick-tempered person does foolish things,
and the one who devises evil schemes is hated.

PROVERBS 14:17 NIV

For wrath killeth the foolish man, and envy slayeth the silly one.

JOB 5:2 KJV

When we pause to meditate, to go to a quiet place to get alone with God and be still, we are choosing to let Him have control in a situation. In going to God about our anger, we open the door for Him to calm us. In handing over our feelings of anger, we make room for peace.

Lord, enable me to trust You wholly with my anger and keep me from sin. Amen.

No one has seen God at any time; if we love one another,
God abides in us, and His love is perfected in us.

1 JOHN 4:12 NASB

When I consider your heavens, the work of your fingers, the moon and the stars,
which you have set in place, what is mankind that you are
mindful of them, human beings that you care for them?

PSALM 8:3–4 NIV

You are important to your heavenly Father, more important than the sun, the moon, and the stars. In fact, He cares so much that He sent His Son, Jesus, to offer His life as a sacrifice for your sins. Now that's love!

Father, who am I that You would think twice about me? And yet You love me, and for that I am eternally grateful. Amen.

Day 278
REFUGE

. . . .

"This God—his way is perfect; the word of the LORD proves true;
he is a shield for all those who take refuge in him."

2 SAMUEL 22:31 ESV

You are my hiding place; you will protect me from trouble
and surround me with songs of deliverance.

PSALM 32:7 NIV

Jesus is your hiding place, a haven, a quietness. Give the Lord your worries, your troubles, and your questions. Give Him your praise and thanksgiving, too. He promises to sing songs of deliverance over you.

J esus, be my refuge. Lift my burdens. Sing songs of deliverance over me, I ask. Amen.

Make it your ambition to lead a quiet life: You should mind your own business and work with your hands, just as we told you, so that your daily life may win the respect of outsiders and so that you will not be dependent on anybody.

1 Thessalonians 4:11–12 niv

Now when the Sabbath was past, Mary Magdalene, Mary the mother of James, and Salome bought spices, that they might come and anoint Him.

Mark 16:1 nkjv

There is spiritual value in the monotonous tasks essential to our lives. Often it's in these times that we are surprised by the Lord. As we engage our bodies in work, our minds are free to feel His presence and sense His leading.

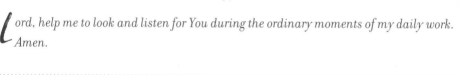

Lord, help me to look and listen for You during the ordinary moments of my daily work. Amen.

Day 280
ADVICE

Listen to advice and accept instruction, that you may gain wisdom in the future.
PROVERBS 19:20 ESV

The heartfelt counsel of a friend is as sweet as perfume and incense.
PROVERBS 27:9 NLT

How encouraging to know that God longs to counsel us—to advise. And He's fully aware that nighttime is hard. Instead of fretting when you climb into bed, use the nighttime as your special time with God. Meet with Him and expect to receive His counsel.

*W*hen the cares of the day overwhelm me, Father, I turn to Your counsel. Instruct my heart. Amen.

RIGHTEOUSNESS

For the LORD is righteous, He loves righteousness; the upright will behold His face.

PSALM 11:7 NASB

"If only there were someone to mediate between us, someone to bring us together, someone to remove God's rod from me, so that his terror would frighten me no more."

JOB 9:33–34 NIV

God knew of our need for someone to bridge the gap between us and our perfect heavenly Father. So He sent Jesus to be our arbitrator and the perfect sacrifice for our sins. Because of His death, we don't have to fear God's wrath.

ord, thank You for sending Jesus to be the bridge between us. Thank You that Christ's righteousness, not mine, saves me. Amen.

Day 282
TRIALS

For you know that the testing of your faith produces steadfastness.

JAMES 1:3 ESV

The spider taketh hold with her hands, and is in kings' palaces.

PROVERBS 30:28 KJV

Life might have knocked us down, but it hasn't knocked us out if we summon what God has put within us. With the power of prayer, we can stand on God's Word and draw forth what we need to rise again.

Father, please allow the Holy Spirit to work in my life. I need Your help through this trial. Amen.

....
....
....
....
....
....
....
....
....
....
....
....

As pressure and stress bear down on me, I find joy in your commands.

PSALM 119:143 NLT

Do not be anxious about anything, but in every situation,
by prayer and petition, with thanksgiving, present your requests to God.

PHILIPPIANS 4:6 NIV

When was the last time you did an anxiety check? After all, we're instructed not to be anxious about anything. Instead, we're to turn to God in prayer so that He can take our burdens. Once they're lifted, it's bye-bye anxiety!

Lord, I don't always remember to check my stress levels. Today I hand my anxieties to You. Amen.

Day 284
SALVATION

If you declare with your mouth, "Jesus is Lord," and believe in your heart that God raised him from the dead, you will be saved. For it is with your heart that you believe and are justified, and it is with your mouth that you profess your faith and are saved.

ROMANS 10:9–10 TNIV

For by grace you have been saved through faith. And this is not your own doing; it is the gift of God, not a result of works, so that no one may boast.

EPHESIANS 2:8–9 ESV

When we know the truth of salvation in Jesus, the burdens of the world that used to be overwhelming are lifted from our shoulders. Real freedom is simply this: God has everything under control, including our salvation.

Jesus, show me how to take hold of my salvation, that I may experience total freedom in You. Amen.

....

....

....

....

....

....

....

....

....

....

....

Anyone who has been stealing must steal no longer, but must work, doing something useful with their own hands, that they may have something to share with those in need.

EPHESIANS 4:28 NIV

If I give all I possess to the poor and give over my body to hardship that I may boast, but do not have love, I gain nothing.

1 CORINTHIANS 13:3 NIV

Jesus told the people that whenever they came to the aid of another person in need, they were aiding Him. Without God we would not possess the things we do. All things come to us from God, and true prosperity comes when we learn to give to others as freely as God gives to us.

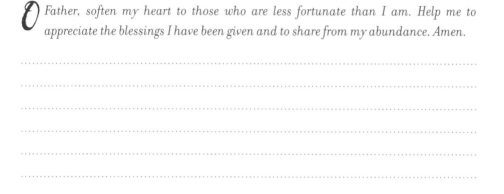

O Father, soften my heart to those who are less fortunate than I am. Help me to appreciate the blessings I have been given and to share from my abundance. Amen.

Day 286
GOD'S PROTECTION

And they shall no more be a prey to the heathen, neither shall the beast of the land devour them; but they shall dwell safely, and none shall make them afraid.

EZEKIEL 34:28 KJV

Though I walk in the midst of trouble, thou wilt revive me: thou shalt stretch forth thine hand against the wrath of mine enemies, and thy right hand shall save me.

PSALM 138:7 KJV

Our health, our safety, our ability to move, to think, and to play, all come from God's power. He is protecting our minds and hearts from evil. He surrounds us with the Holy Spirit. God is aware of every detail of our lives and is carefully tending us.

Thank You, God, for preserving me. Help me to remember that I am valuable to You and You are concerned with every detail of my life. Amen.

*Israel, I will teach you. My words will be like gentle rain on tender young plants,
or like dew on the grass.*

DEUTERONOMY 32:2 CEV

Gracious words are a honeycomb, sweet to the soul and healing to the bones.

PROVERBS 16:24 NIV

Our words should reflect the presence of God in our hearts. Only the most excellent and right things should spring forth from our mouths.

*Let me build up, rather than tear down. May my speech reflect my great love for You,
Lord. Amen.*

Day 288
HEALTH

Lord, make me to know mine end, and the measure of my days, what it is: that I may know how frail I am. Behold, thou hast made my days as an handbreadth; and mine age is as nothing before thee.

PSALM 39:4–5 KJV

Is any sick among you? let him call for the elders of the church; and let them pray over him, anointing him with oil in the name of the Lord: and the prayer of faith shall save the sick, and the Lord shall raise him up.

JAMES 5:14–15 KJV

Investment in exercising, getting enough sleep, and eating properly reaps countless benefits in helping us be more productive, clearheaded, and energetic. God created our bodies as temples, and we only get one.

Father, thank You for my temple. Help me to care for it to the best of my ability and honor You with healthy habits. Amen.

*But You, O Lord, know me [and understand my devotion to You]; You see me;
And You examine the attitude of my heart toward You. Drag out the faithless like
sheep for the slaughter [O Lord] And set them apart for the day of slaughter.*

JEREMIAH 12:3 AMP

*Therefore, my dear brothers and sisters, stand firm. Let nothing move you.
Always give yourselves fully to the work of the Lord, because you know
that your labor in the Lord is not in vain.*

1 CORINTHIANS 15:58 NIV

It's not only possible to stand firm during tough times, it's what God expects. He doesn't want anything to move us. Today if you're faced with challenges, resolve to stand firm—no matter what. Remain committed to the faith.

Lord, give me the spiritual backbone to stand firm, to remain committed to You. . .no matter what. Amen.

....
....
....
....
....
....
....
....
....
....

Day 290
PERSEVERANCE

*As you know, we count as blessed those who have persevered. You have heard
of Job's perseverance and have seen what the Lord finally brought
about. The Lord is full of compassion and mercy.*

JAMES 5:11 NIV

*You need to persevere so that when you have done the will of God,
you will receive what he has promised.*

HEBREWS 10:36 TNIV

Our world is upside down. To be good is foreign or alien to the majority. The key is
not to give up. The Lord will reward those who persevere in the face of frustration.
God loves the pure in heart, and it is well worth it to hold on for His sake.

*Be with me, Lord, to strengthen me, and to help me deal with people who think wrong
is right. I want to be Your child, not a child of the world. Amen.*

The LORD is truthful; he can be trusted.

PSALM 33:4 CEV

Send out your light and your truth; let them lead me;
let them bring me to your holy hill and to your dwelling!

PSALM 43:3 ESV

The world is full of darkness and confusion. God's enemies would have us believe there is no such thing as absolute truth, no difference between right and wrong. But God's Word tells us otherwise. God's truth brings freedom to our lives that in turn produces joy.

esus, cause me to remember that all truth and all light come from You. Amen.

Day 292
GOD'S PROVISION

. . . .

Take no thought for your life, what ye shall eat, or what ye shall drink; nor yet for your body, what ye shall put on. Is not the life more than meat, and the body than raiment? Behold the fowls of the air: for they sow not, neither do they reap, nor gather into barns; yet your heavenly Father feedeth them. Are ye not much better than they?

MATTHEW 6:25–26 KJV

"For all the animals of the forest are mine, and I own the cattle on a thousand hills."

PSALM 50:10 NLT

God's resources are vast and He has promised to meet all our needs. We can depend on Him to provide for us; you do not have a need that God cannot meet. Rest in the knowledge that God will take care of you.

Heavenly Father, thank You for being my Provider. Amen.

. . . .
. . . .
. . . .
. . . .
. . . .
. . . .
. . . .
. . . .
. . . .
. . . .
. . . .
. . . .

SPIRITUAL GROWTH

Like newborn infants, long for the pure spiritual milk,
that by it you may grow up into salvation.

1 Peter 2:2 esv

Therefore, my dear friends, as you have always obeyed—not only in my presence,
but now much more in my absence—continue to work out your salvation with fear
and trembling, for it is God who works in you to will and to
act in order to fulfill his good purpose.

Philippians 2:12–13 niv

Spiritual growth doesn't just happen—it takes a lot of discipline. Reading God's Word is a great start, but we must take it a step further. We need to transfer our head knowledge to the heart by applying God's truth in everyday life.

Dear Lord, remind me of the importance of spiritual growth—in this life and eternity to come. Amen.

Day 294
REBELLION

He turned the sea into dry land; they passed through the river on foot.
There did we rejoice in him, who rules by his might forever,
whose eyes keep watch on the nations—let not the rebellious exalt themselves.

PSALM 66:6–7 ESV

Where there is no revelation, the people cast off restraint;
but happy is he who keeps the law.

PROVERBS 29:18 NKJV

The law was given for our good, to lead us to Christ and to instruct us in how to live. Even though we fail daily in keeping all of it, we have the assurance that Christ has kept it for us. When we do not focus on Christ, we will cast off all restraint, rebelling against the very things that are good for us.

Father, keep my eyes focused on You. Enable me by Your Spirit to love and keep Your law. Amen.

"But if a wicked person turns away from all the sins they have committed and keeps all my decrees and does what is just and right, that person will surely live; they will not die."

EZEKIEL 18:21 NIV

"Come, let us return to the LORD. He has torn us to pieces; now he will heal us. He has injured us; now he will bandage our wounds."

HOSEA 6:1 NLT

When we sin, it is a private matter between God and ourselves. Take your sins before God, repent for each one, and glory in the grace of God, by which we receive full pardon for all we do wrong.

Forgive me, Lord. Make a new creation out of this old soul. Prepare me for the kingdom to come each day of my life. Amen.

Day 296
APPEARANCE

*And being found in appearance as a man, he humbled himself by
becoming obedient to death—even death on a cross!*

PHILIPPIANS 2:8 NIV

*But the LORD said to Samuel, "Don't judge by his appearance or height,
for I have rejected him. The LORD doesn't see things the way you see them.
People judge by outward appearance, but the LORD looks at the heart."*

1 SAMUEL 16:7 NLT

Where we humans make snap judgments about others by their appearance, God
looks deep into our hearts. Make it a priority to value others—and yourself—for the
appearance of the heart.

*Dear Father, thank You for being a God who values me for far more than my physical
appearance. Help me always to look at others with the same depth. Amen.*

The Lord knoweth how to deliver the godly out of temptations.

2 Peter 2:9 kjv

*How long must I wrestle with my thoughts and day after day have sorrow in my heart?
How long will my enemy triumph over me?*

Psalm 13:2 niv

Every day we struggle with thoughts that may not be pleasing to God. Your mind is a battlefield. That's why we are advised to bring every thought captive. Instead of wrestling with your thoughts, make a conscious effort to give your thought life to the One capable of handling it.

Father, sometimes I don't like the thoughts flitting through my mind. Today I give my thoughts to You. Amen.

. . . .

. . . .

. . . .

. . . .

. . . .

. . . .

. . . .

. . . .

. . . .

. . . .

. . . .

. . . .

Day 298
WORSHIP

....

You are my God. I worship you. In my heart, I long for you,
as I would long for a stream in a scorching desert.

PSALM 63:1 CEV

Worship the LORD in the splendor of his holiness; tremble before him, all the earth.

PSALM 96:9 NIV

There's great joy in lifting up praises to God. And He loves it when you come into His presence with singing. If you're not convinced, read the book of Psalms!

O Father, You've been so good to me! Today the song in my heart erupts. I'll make a joyful noise because of Your goodness.

*No one knows the day or hour. The angels in heaven don't know,
and the Son himself doesn't know. Only the Father knows.*

MATTHEW 24:36 CEV

*And God said, "Let there be lights in the expanse of the heavens to separate the day from
the night. And let them be for signs and for seasons, and for days and years."*

GENESIS 1:14 ESV

We may dwell too much in the past or worry too much about our future. Think about
God's hands that hold our time. Our moments to our years are in the hands of the
creator, healer, sustainer, provider, redeemer, and lover of our souls.

*Gracious God who rules and reigns over all my days, cause me to remember that I am
held by Your loving hands—always. Amen.*

. . . .
. . . .
. . . .
. . . .
. . . .
. . . .
. . . .
. . . .
. . . .
. . . .
. . . .
. . . .

Day 300
IDOLS

. . . .

What is an idol worth? It's merely a false god. Why trust a speechless image made from wood or metal by human hands?

HABAKKUK 2:18 CEV

Do any of the worthless idols of the nations bring rain? Do the skies themselves send down showers? No, it is you, LORD our God. Therefore our hope is in you, for you are the one who does all this.

JEREMIAH 14:22 NIV

Compared to God, the wood and stone idols in the Bible are useless. Similarly, when we trust someone or something other than God, then we trust something as useless as wood and stone idols.

Lord, help me rely on You—and not things that cannot provide the comfort, protection, and salvation I need. Amen.

. . . .

. . . .

. . . .

. . . .

. . . .

. . . .

. . . .

. . . .

. . . .

. . . .

*The man knew what each servant could do. So he handed five thousand coins
to the first servant, two thousand to the second, and one thousand to the third.
Then he left the country. As soon as the man had gone, the servant with
the five thousand coins used them to earn five thousand more.*

MATTHEW 25:15–16 CEV

*Whoever loves pleasure will become poor;
whoever loves wine and olive oil will never be rich.*

PROVERBS 21:17 NIV

Most of us can relate to the temptation to spend more than we have. Saying no takes wisdom and discipline. But wise spending decisions bring peace and security, especially during tough economic times.

Father, help me to spend my money wisely. Amen.

Day 302
GRIEF

. . . .

Surely our griefs He Himself bore, and our sorrows He carried.

Isaiah 53:4 nasb

For his anger lasts only a moment, but his favor lasts a lifetime;
weeping may stay for the night, but rejoicing comes in the morning.

Psalm 30:5 niv

Times of true mourning don't last forever. They may feel like they do, but they eventually pass. Hang tight to the One who can best minister to your broken heart. He wants you to know that your pain and your tears will only last for a season. Joy is coming.

God, thank You for Your healing balm. I'm so grateful that my tears are only temporary. Amen.

It's smart to be patient, but it's stupid to lose your temper.

PROVERBS 14:29 CEV

Whoever is slow to anger is better than the mighty,
and he who rules his spirit than he who takes a city.

PROVERBS 16:32 ESV

Rather than letting the fire in your heart spew from your tongue, take your hurt to the Lord before you speak. Ask Him to help you to forgive. Forgiveness squelches anger like throwing cold water on a fire, and through forgiveness God is glorified in your life.

Dear Lord, help me deal with anger when it first arises in my heart. Amen.

....

....

....

....

....

....

....

....

....

....

....

....

....

....

Day 304
JOY

···

When anxiety was great within me, your consolation brought me joy.
PSALM 94:19 NIV

I'm thanking you, GOD, from a full heart, I'm writing the book on your wonders.
I'm whistling, laughing, and jumping for joy; I'm singing your song, High God.
PSALM 9:1–2 MSG

Have you ever experienced joy that couldn't be contained? Such joy rises from a heart filled with hope. You feel like telling everyone just what God has done for you. Celebrate the victories you've experienced, large or small. Jump for joy!

L ord, my heart is overwhelmed with joy. You've done so much for me, and I don't deserve it. Thank You! Amen.

"Abide in Me, and I in you. As the branch cannot bear fruit of itself, unless it abides in the vine, neither can you, unless you abide in Me. I am the vine, you are the branches. He who abides in Me, and I in him, bears much fruit; for without Me you can do nothing."

JOHN 15:4–5 NKJV

Now he who keeps His commandments abides in Him, and He in him. And by this we know that He abides in us, by the Spirit whom He has given us.

1 JOHN 3:24 NKJV

Abiding in God means we trust in Him and live with our entire lives centered on our Lord. This is more than lip-service "faith"; it means putting our money where our mouths are when we face everyday difficulties.

May my life be more than surface-level faith to You, Lord. Be my focus. Amen.

....
....
....
....
....
....
....
....
....
....
....
....
....

Day 306
ANGELS

....

*The angel of the L*ORD *encampeth round about them that fear him, and delivereth them.*

PSALM 34:7 KJV

For he shall give his angels charge over thee, to keep thee in all thy ways.
They shall bear thee up in their hands, lest thou dash thy foot against a stone.

PSALM 91:11–12 KJV

Who's to say where God's angels are? Perhaps we each have an angel who watches us and guides us. God, in His love for us, has set the angels over us. Rest secure. The angels are watching.

*H*elp me to believe in the angels that You send, Lord. I need watching over. I need You to be with me. Amen.

....
....
....
....
....
....
....
....
....
....
....
....

Ah Lord God! behold, thou hast made the heaven and the earth by thy great power and stretched out arm, and there is nothing too hard for thee.

JEREMIAH 32:17 KJV

But it is good for me to draw near to God: I have put my trust in the Lord God, that I may declare all thy works.

PSALM 73:28 KJV

Trust is a tricky thing. It is difficult to put our trust in others, because we can't be sure whether they will value it. That fear should not apply when it comes to putting our trust in God. He will follow us to the ends of the earth to make sure we know of His great love.

*W*herever I go, Lord, I need to know that You are with me. I will put my trust in You, knowing that You will always do what is best for me. Help me to trust You more each day. Amen.

Day 308
ADDICTION

· ·

Jesus answered them, "Truly, truly, I say to you,
everyone who commits sin is the slave of sin."

JOHN 8:34 NASB

When you follow the desires of your sinful nature, the results are very clear: sexual
immorality, impurity, lustful pleasures, idolatry, sorcery, hostility, quarreling, jealousy,
outbursts of anger, selfish ambition, dissension, division, envy, drunkenness,
wild parties, and other sins like these. Let me tell you again, as I have before,
that anyone living that sort of life will not inherit the Kingdom of God.

GALATIANS 5:19–21 NLT

Scripture does not mention many specific addictions like gambling or drugs, but it
clearly sets forth principles that make it clear that believers should not engage in an
addictive lifestyle.

Lord, help me avoid addiction in my life, I pray. And should I find myself straying from
Your commands, lead me back to Your love. Amen.

· ·

· ·

· ·

· ·

· ·

· ·

· ·

· ·

· ·

Where there is no guidance the people fall,
but in abundance of counselors there is victory.

PROVERBS 11:14 NASB

The wise will hear and increase their learning, And the person of understanding
will acquire wise counsel and the skill [to steer his course
wisely and lead others to the truth].

PROVERBS 1:5 AMP

Wisdom comes from God, not people. But those who walk closely with Him can be good advisers when we need help. No one should avoid getting good advice when it's needed, and going first to God, then to godly humans, will lead us into wise decisions.

ord, help me to seek godly advice. Amen.

Day 310
ARGUMENT

But now you must stop doing such things. You must quit being angry, hateful, and evil. You must no longer say insulting or cruel things about others.

COLOSSIANS 3:8 CEV

Good sense makes one slow to anger, and it is his glory to overlook an offense.

PROVERBS 19:11 ESV

There is enough argument and strife in the world without Christians adding to it senselessly. It is not enough that Christians try to do good. It is also vital that they always strive to do no harm.

Lord God, help me to do good to those around me and guard me that I do no harm. Amen.

For, as I have often told you before and now tell you again even with tears, many live as enemies of the cross of Christ. Their destiny is destruction, their god is their stomach, and their glory is in their shame. Their mind is set on earthly things.

PHILIPPIANS 3:18–19 NIV

For if after they have escaped the pollutions of the world through the knowledge of the Lord and Saviour Jesus Christ, they are again entangled therein, and overcome, the latter end is worse with them than the beginning. For it had been better for them not to have known the way of righteousness, than, after they have known it, to turn from the holy commandment delivered unto them.

2 PETER 2:20–21 KJV

All other paths lead to destruction and pain. How wonderful it is to know that the road to God is never blocked. We cannot do anything to make God stop loving us.

I never want to be without You in my life, Lord. Thank You for remaining even as I stray. Amen.

. . . .

. . . .

. . . .

. . . .

. . . .

. . . .

. . . .

. . . .

. . . .

. . . .

Day 312
PRAISE

*I thank you from my heart, and I will never stop singing your praises,
my Lord and my God.*

Psalm 30:12 cev

*But you are a chosen generation, a royal priesthood, a holy nation, His own special
people, that you may proclaim the praises of Him who called you
out of darkness into His marvelous light.*

1 Peter 2:9 nkjv

As Christians, we are people of praise. Every prayer we offer unto God should acknowledge the many wonderful things He has done for us. God gives good things to His children, and we should be thankful for all that we have.

Lord, I cannot believe how much I have been given. Help open my eyes to the many blessings that have been bestowed upon me. Make me thankful, Lord. Amen.

....
....
....
....
....
....
....
....
....
....
....

*I will bless the LORD at all times; His praise shall continually be in my mouth.
My soul will make its boast in the LORD; the humble will hear it and rejoice.*

PSALM 34:1–2 NASB

The godly always give generous loans to others, and their children are a blessing.

PSALM 37:26 NLT

If our only blessings were possessions, in heaven we would be the poorest of souls. But because God made Himself our best blessing, we are rich both here and for eternity.

Father, when I forget the wonderful blessings You bestow, remind me of the greatest blessing—Your Son, Jesus Christ.

Day 314
CHURCH

God has put all things under the authority of Christ and has made him head over all things for the benefit of the church. And the church is his body; it is made full and complete by Christ, who fills all things everywhere with himself.

EPHESIANS 1:22–23 NLT

We will speak the truth in love, growing in every way more and more like Christ, who is the head of his body, the church. He makes the whole body fit together perfectly. As each part does its own special work, it helps the other parts grow, so that the whole body is healthy and growing and full of love.

EPHESIANS 4:15–16 NLT

Because He dwells in them and works out His plan through them, God's people are His church. Wherever people who love Him are gathered together, God is there.

Father, as I gather together with other believers in communion, I pray we are a reflection of Your church. Amen.

Work for the things that make peace and help each other become stronger Christians.

ROMANS 14:19 NLV

*"If he walks in My statutes and My ordinances so as to deal faithfully—
he is righteous and will surely live," declares the Lord GOD.*

EZEKIEL 18:9 NASB

Too many people think that being a Christian means believing but not doing. Being a Christian means living a godly life and rejecting many things that the world says are okay.

I live with a foot in two worlds, Lord. Reach out and pull me into the kingdom, that I might step from this world into Yours. Amen.

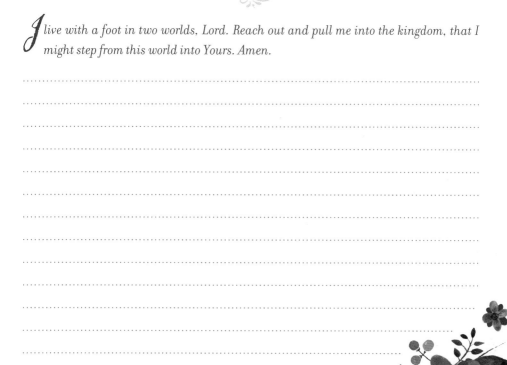

Day 316
COMFORT

· ·

*And it shall come to pass in the day that the L*ORD *shall give thee rest from thy sorrow, and from thy fear, and from the hard bondage wherein thou wast made to serve.*

ISAIAH 14:3 KJV

For the Lord himself shall descend from heaven with a shout, with the voice of the archangel, and with the trump of God: and the dead in Christ shall rise first: then we which are alive and remain shall be caught up together with them in the clouds, to meet the Lord in the air: and so shall we ever be with the Lord. Wherefore comfort one another with these words.

1 THESSALONIANS 4:16–18 KJV

The Word of God can be a powerful source of comfort for us. In times of danger and dread, the Lord will come close to us, to comfort and protect us. Rest in the Lord, and He will save you.

Heavenly Father, thank You for Your comforting words. May I draw near to them always. Amen.

· ·
· ·
· ·
· ·
· ·
· ·
· ·
· ·

· ·

*It's certainly possible to say, "Other branches were pruned so that I could be grafted in!"
Well and good. But they were pruned because they were deadwood, no longer connected
by belief and commitment to the root. The only reason you're on the tree is because
your graft "took" when you believed, and because you're connected to that belief-
nurturing root. So don't get cocky and strut your branch. Be humbly
mindful of the root that keeps you lithe and green.*

ROMANS 11:19–20 MSG

*I am saying this for your own good, not to restrict you,
but that you may live in a right way in undivided devotion to the Lord.*

1 CORINTHIANS 7:35 NIV

God doesn't want worthy people nearly as much as He wants committed people.
Those individuals who stand up and say, "Here am I, Lord! Take me," are the ones
who please Him most.

I want to give my all to You, Lord. Make me a reflection of Your divine light. Amen.

· ·
· ·
· ·
· ·
· ·
· ·
· ·
· ·
· ·
· ·
· ·

Day 318
COMPASSION

*Just as a father has compassion on his children,
so the Lord has compassion on those who fear Him.*

PSALM 103:13 NASB

*So the Lord must wait for you to come to him so he can show you his love and
compassion. For the Lord is a faithful God. Blessed are those who wait for his help.*

ISAIAH 30:18 NLT

In a rough-and-tumble world, there's great need for compassion. Hurting people seek it and often receive the hardness of this world instead. Compassion is one of Christianity's hallmarks. When we offer it to others, we reflect God's love and draw sinners to Him.

I want to touch hearts for Christ. Help me, Father, to radiate the gentle, tender virtue of compassion in this world. Amen.

And God said, Let us make man in our image, after our likeness: and let them have dominion over the fish of the sea, and over the fowl of the air, and over the cattle, and over all the earth, and over every creeping thing that creepeth upon the earth.

GENESIS 1:26 KJV

The Scriptures say, "The earth and everything in it belong to the Lord."

1 CORINTHIANS 10:26 CEV

God has given us the earth to have dominion over it. We must remember that this is the only place we have to live in and treat it accordingly.

Lord, when I take this earth for granted, remind me of Your care for Your creation. Help me to care for the world as You do. Amen.

Day 320
CORRUPTION

*"If I say to corruption, 'You are my father,' and to the worm, 'My mother'
or 'My sister,' where then is my hope—who can see any hope for me?"*

JOB 17:14–15 NIV

*God made great and marvelous promises, so that his nature would become part of us.
Then we could escape our evil desires and the corrupt influences of this world.*

2 PETER 1:4 CEV

It is frightening to listen to the decrees made by some of our world leaders. If it were true that they really had the ultimate power, there would be no reason for hope. We know better, however. The only true power in this world is the power of God, and our fate will not be decided by men and women, but by God.

Father God, hear the prayers of Your people, and give us peace and confidence of a bright new age to come. Amen.

"For behold, I create new heavens and a new earth;
and the former shall not be remembered or come to mind."

ISAIAH 65:17 NKJV

The LORD is good to everyone. He showers compassion on all his creation.

PSALM 145:9 NLT

Human beings in all their wisdom and genius have created nothing to compare with the least of God's creations. His power, might, and majesty humble us and help us to remember that He alone is God.

how forth Your might through Your creations, O Lord. Remind me of Your greatness and power throughout the day. You are wonderful, Lord! Amen.

Day 322
DEATH

....

When calamity comes, the wicked are brought down,
but even in death the righteous seek refuge in God.

PROVERBS 14:32 NIV

For this is God, our God forever and ever; He will be our guide even to death.

PSALM 48:14 NKJV

We often hope that we can leave a legacy, a testament to our life, after we die. There is no more fitting legacy than helping other people learn to love life and enjoy it every day.

Father, I pray that my life is a reflection of You so that others embrace the joy I have been given. Amen.

....
....
....
....
....
....
....
....
....
....
....
....
....

Where there is no guidance, a people falls,
but in an abundance of counselors there is safety.

PROVERBS 11:14 ESV

A good name is rather to be chosen than great riches,
and loving favour rather than silver and gold.

PROVERBS 22:1 KJV

When it comes to decision making, we need to ask ourselves, Who do I get advice from? If our primary counselor is not God, we may be headed for trouble. But He also puts wise people in our paths. Are we making the most of their advice?

Father, be my first source when I am faced with a decision. Lead me to others who will guide me in Your way. Amen.

Day 324
COMMITMENT

So let's keep focused on that goal, those of us who want everything God has for us. If any of you have something else in mind, something less than total commitment, God will clear your blurred vision—you'll see it yet! Now that we're on the right track, let's stay on it.

PHILIPPIANS 3:15–16 MSG

My love be with all of you in Christ Jesus. Amen.

1 CORINTHIANS 16:24 AMP

God is not someone that we should turn to only in times of trial. He should be a part of our whole life, both in good times and bad. We must be sure to include God in everything we do.

D ear God, forgive those times when I seem to forget You. Help me to include You in all I do, think, and feel. Amen.

But take diligent heed to do the commandment and the law, which Moses the servant of the LORD charged you, to love the LORD your God, and to walk in all his ways, and to keep his commandments, and to cleave unto him, and to serve him with all your heart and with all your soul.

JOSHUA 22:5 KJV

Keep thy heart with all diligence; for out of it are the issues of life.

PROVERBS 4:23 KJV

When something is the desire of our heart, it should possess us totally. How many of us pursue God with the same diligence?

Help me to pursue You in all ways at all times, O Lord. I want You to be the desire of my heart. Amen.

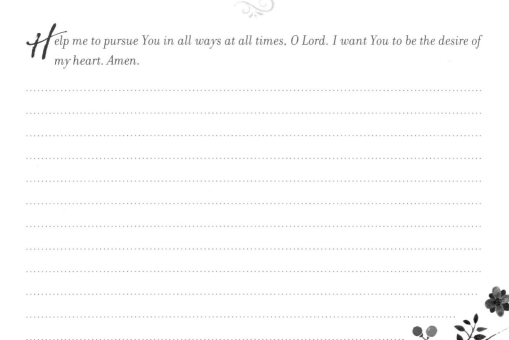

Day 326
DOUBT

When doubts filled my mind, your comfort gave me renewed hope and cheer.

PSALM 94:19 NLT

Jesus answered and said unto them, Verily I say unto you, If ye have faith, and doubt not, ye shall not only do this which is done to the fig tree, but also if ye shall say unto this mountain, Be thou removed, and be thou cast into the sea; it shall be done. And all things, whatsoever ye shall ask in prayer, believing, ye shall receive.

MATTHEW 21:21–22 KJV

Doubt comes to us easily. It is during those times that it is most important to hold fast to the promises of God.

*A*lmighty God, forgive me when I doubt Your will and guidance. Help me always to have the faith I need to trust and obey. Amen.

For you have made the LORD, my refuge, even the Most High, your dwelling place.
No evil will befall you, nor will any plague come near your tent. For He will
give His angels charge concerning you, to guard you in all your ways.

PSALM 91:9–11 NASB

The LORD will keep you from all evil; he will keep your life. The LORD will keep
your going out and your coming in from this time forth and forevermore.

PSALM 121:7–8 ESV

Evil is as oppressive as a thick cloud of smoke. It envelops people and chokes them.
One day the Lord will dispel all evil as a fan dispels smoke. On that day, all God's
people will breathe richly of the fragrance of God.

ord, send the breath of Your Spirit to cleanse me of all evil. Free me from the oppression
of all that I have done wrong, through Your blessed forgiveness. Amen.

. . . .
. . . .
. . . .
. . . .
. . . .
. . . .
. . . .
. . . .
. . . .
. . . .
. . . .

Day 328
EXTRAMARITAL SEX

Now the body is not for sexual immorality but for the Lord, and the Lord for the body.

1 Corinthians 6:13 nkjv

Marriage should be honored by all, and the marriage bed kept pure,
for God will judge the adulterer and all the sexually immoral.

Hebrews 13:4 niv

Adultery undermines the ultimate plan of God that a man and woman will join together in order that the two shall become one in spirit, mind, and body. It trades in the promise of eternal bliss for a moment of physical pleasure.

Lift me up, Father, and raise me high above sin and temptation. Your design is perfect; help me to follow Your will in my marriage. Amen.

. . . .

Then Jesus told him, "You believe because you have seen me.
Blessed are those who believe without seeing me."

JOHN 20:29 NLT

And Jesus said unto them, I am the bread of life: he that cometh to me shall
never hunger; and he that believeth on me shall never thirst.

JOHN 6:35 KJV

We all face decisions about whether to trust God. But the struggle to avoid unbelief is worth it all when we see the benefits of trusting Jesus and experience His love.

Lord, when my human understanding causes me to lack belief, fill me with Your promises that I might believe anew. Amen.

. . . .
. . . .
. . . .
. . . .
. . . .
. . . .
. . . .
. . . .
. . . .
. . . .
. . . .
. . . .
. . . .

Day 330
POVERTY

∙ ∙

"For they all put in out of their surplus, but she, out of her poverty,
put in all she owned, all she had to live on."

MARK 12:44 NASB

The stingy are eager to get rich and are unaware that poverty awaits them.

PROVERBS 28:22 NIV

To come before Jesus means to come before the needy of this world. Jesus said unless you do good unto your brothers and sisters, you have not done good unto Him. Let us join with our Lord in being saviors to a world in need.

Forgive me for wrong priorities, Lord. I worship often in word, but not in deed. Let my actions reinforce the faith I confess with my heart. Amen.

"A family splintered by feuding will fall apart."

LUKE 11:17 NLT

So I bow in prayer before the Father from whom every family
in heaven and on earth gets its true name.

EPHESIANS 3:14–15 NCV

In homes where Christ is King and ruler, it is easy to feel God's blessing. There is no conflict or problem that can upset the blessing that God puts upon a faithful household.

C ome, O Lord, to be the head of my household and the unifier in my family. Amen.

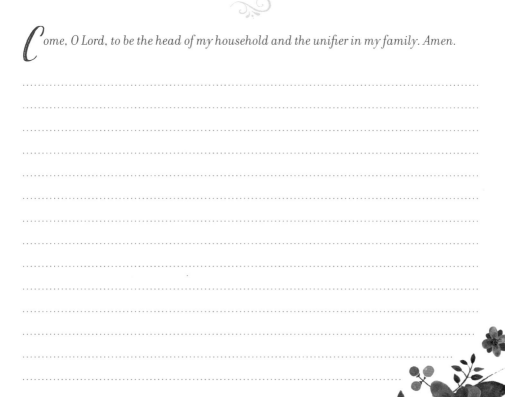

Day 332

FEAR

....

*"Don't fear: I am First, I am Last, I'm Alive. I died,
but I came to life, and my life is now forever."*

REVELATION 1:17–18 MSG

*"And do not fear those who kill the body but cannot kill the soul. But rather fear
Him who is able to destroy both soul and body in hell. Are not two sparrows sold for
a copper coin? And not one of them falls to the ground apart from your Father's will.
But the very hairs of your head are all numbered. Do not fear
therefore; you are of more value than many sparrows."*

MATTHEW 10:28–31 NKJV

Fear of God is a good thing because it draws us closer to Him in respect and love. But
doubtful fears show our lack of reliance on Him.

*Lord, with You I have nothing to fear. When doubtful fear creeps into my life, remind me
of Your power and faithfulness. Amen.*

....

....

....

....

....

....

....

....

....

....

The Lord is a jealous and avenging God; the Lord is avenging and wrathful; the Lord takes vengeance on his adversaries and keeps wrath for his enemies.

NAHUM 1:2 ESV

Never take your own revenge, beloved, but leave room for the wrath of God, for it is written, "VENGEANCE IS MINE, I WILL REPAY," says the Lord.

ROMANS 12:19 NASB

A lot of people live for revenge. They hold grudges, let them burn inside, then explode forth to do whatever damage they can. When someone wrongs you, your duty is to forgive, not to punish.

Heavenly Father, pride often causes me to plot in my heart against those who have wronged me. Create in my heart a spirit of forgiveness instead. Amen.

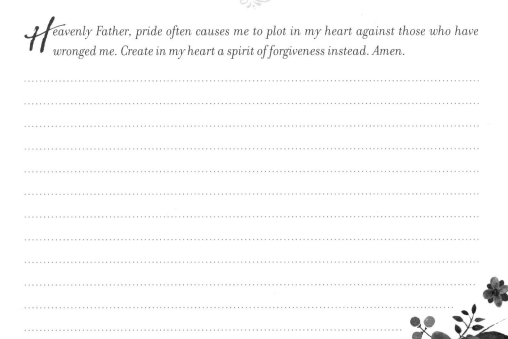

Day 334
RECOGNITION

If you live right, the reward is a good life.

PROVERBS 10:16 CEV

In the future there is laid up for me the crown of righteousness, which the Lord,
the righteous Judge, will award to me on that day; and not only to me,
but also to all who have loved His appearing.

2 TIMOTHY 4:8 NASB

Truly faithful people don't have to go seeking acclaim. When we pursue recognition, we open ourselves to failure and disgrace. We should focus on the work we need to do rather than the credit we will receive for doing it.

*D*estroy in me, O Lord, the desire to do things that make me look good. Rather, let me do things for Your glory. Amen.

My eyes long for your salvation and for the fulfillment of your righteous promise.

PSALM 119:123 ESV

Now if their transgression is riches for the world and their failure is riches for the Gentiles, how much more will their fulfillment be!

ROMANS 11:12 NASB

Life is a privilege that God wants us to value. When we turn from Him and pursue our own selfish desires, we lose sight of the sacredness of His gift. We may think that we can find fulfillment in life on our own, but it is through God and God alone that we can come to know the wonder of life most fully.

Help me to see the beauty and wonder of this life You have given to me, O Lord. Amen.

Day 336
GOD'S CORRECTION

. . . .

For they verily for a few days chastened us after their own pleasure; but he for our profit, that we might be partakers of his holiness. Now no chastening for the present seemeth to be joyous, but grievous: nevertheless afterward it yieldeth the peaceable fruit of righteousness unto them which are exercised thereby.

HEBREWS 12:10–11 KJV

As many as I love, I rebuke and chasten: be zealous therefore, and repent.

REVELATION 3:19 KJV

Often we know what God says, but we do other things instead. When we find ourselves in trouble, we look to God to bail us out, then wonder why He doesn't jump to our aid. Sometimes God allows us to struggle through adversity in order to learn that He means what He says.

*D*ear heavenly Father, I so often do what I know You do not want me to do. Forgive my disobedience. Help me to heed Your will, not my own. Amen.

. . . .

. . . .

. . . .

. . . .

. . . .

. . . .

. . . .

. . . .

. . . .

And suddenly, a woman who had a flow of blood for twelve years came from behind and touched the hem of His garment. For she said to herself, "If only I may touch His garment, I shall be made well." But Jesus turned around, and when He saw her He said, "Be of good cheer, daughter; your faith has made you well."

MATTHEW 9:20–22 NKJV

And the prayer offered in faith will make the sick person well; the Lord will raise them up. If they have sinned, they will be forgiven. Therefore confess your sins to each other and pray for each other so that you may be healed.

JAMES 5:15–16 NIV

Whether it's for our bodies or our spirits, we all need God's healing touch. And God is always willing to offer it to us. Look how often Jesus healed during His ministry—not only hurting bodies but also souls that had been severely damaged.

ord, Your Word displays a longing to heal. Touch my heart today, that I may be healed. Amen.

Day 338
RIGHTEOUSNESS

Your righteousness is like the highest mountains, your justice like the great deep.

Psalm 36:6 niv

Because I have sinned against him, I will bear the Lord's wrath, until he pleads my case and upholds my cause. He will bring me out into the light; I will see his righteousness.

Micah 7:9 niv

Through the death and resurrection of Jesus, Christ's righteousness becomes the righteousness of all who believe in Him and turn their hearts over to Him. Jesus paid the penalty that would have come to us. We have no fear of condemnation. All we have is the promise of love and forgiveness.

Though I do not deserve Your great love, Father God, I thank You that You give it so freely. Embrace me as Your child, and help me remember that I am Yours. Amen.

And I will cleanse them from all their iniquity, whereby they have sinned against me, and I will pardon all their iniquities, whereby they have sinned, and whereby they have transgressed against me.

JEREMIAH 33:8 KJV

But if we walk in the light, as he is in the light, we have fellowship one with another, and the blood of Jesus Christ his Son cleanseth us from all sin.

1 JOHN 1:7 KJV

Too often we come before the Lord with the feeling that we shouldn't be there. True, we have sinned, but God does not want us to dwell on the fact that we have sinned, but that we have been forgiven.

Your grace has made me worthy, Lord. What I could not do on my own, You have done for me. Thank You, Father, from the depths of my soul. Amen.

Day 340
GOD'S OMNISCIENCE

. . . .

Be not ye therefore like unto them:
for your Father knoweth what things ye have need of, before ye ask him.

MATTHEW 6:8 KJV

This then is the message which we have heard of him, and declare unto you,
that God is light, and in him is no darkness at all.

1 JOHN 1:5 KJV

From the very beginning of time, God has had each and every one of us in His mind. He knows us completely. There is never even one moment when we are out of God's vision.

Heavenly Father, You are amazing! I am just one, but I am always in Your care. Amen.

He guides me along the right paths for his name's sake.

PSALM 23:3 NIV

Guide me in your truth and teach me,
for you are God my Savior, and my hope is in you all day long.

PSALM 25:5 NIV

God has given us a conscience, a "still small voice," an inner wisdom that guides us and comforts us when we remain true to its instruction.

O heavenly Father, I reach out to Your guidance and will. Help me to listen for Your instruction. Amen.

Day 342
GOD'S PROTECTION

∙∙∙

All of you worship the Lord, so you must trust him to help and protect you.

PSALM 115:11 CEV

The Lord shall preserve thee from all evil: he shall preserve thy soul. The Lord shall preserve thy going out and thy coming in from this time forth, and even for evermore.

PSALM 121:7–8 KJV

If we will set our sights on the Lord, He will make our steps sure. No snare, trap, or pitfall can stop us when our eyes are on the Lord. He will guard us each step of the way.

I am uncertain, Lord, and often afraid. Instill Your holy confidence in me. I place my trust in Your protection, that I might walk a good walk of faith and never stumble. Amen.

Or what man is there of you, whom if his son ask bread, will he give him a stone?
Or if he ask a fish, will he give him a serpent? If ye then, being evil, know how to
give good gifts unto your children, how much more shall your Father
which is in heaven give good things to them that ask him?

MATTHEW 7:9–11 KJV

I have provided all kinds of fruit and grain for you to eat.

GENESIS 1:29 CEV

God has given good things to His children, and when one thing doesn't work out, we can rest assured that something else is soon to come along. In good and bad, the Lord is with us, helping us make the best of things.

You give so many good things, Lord. Help me to see past the things that are wrong. Thank You for providing the support I need. Amen.

....
....
....
....
....
....
....
....
....
....
....
....

Day 344
GRACE

. . . .

Being made right with God by his grace,
we could have the hope of receiving the life that never ends
TITUS 3:7 NCV

But when grace is shown to the wicked, they do not learn righteousness; even in a land
of uprightness they go on doing evil and do not regard the majesty of the LORD.
ISAIAH 26:10 NIV

It is through God's grace that we can avoid the pain that sin brings. It is in His will that we find the path that leads to true happiness.

*D**ear Lord, let me know that I can be forgiven for the things I do wrong, and that I can start afresh if I will just focus my eyes and my soul on You. Amen.*

. . . .
. . . .
. . . .
. . . .
. . . .
. . . .
. . . .
. . . .
. . . .
. . . .
. . . .
. . . .
. . . .

*As ye have therefore received Christ Jesus the Lord, so walk ye in him:
Rooted and built up in him, and stablished in the faith, as ye have been
taught, abounding therein with thanksgiving.*

COLOSSIANS 2:6–7 KJV

*And whatsoever ye do in word or deed, do all in the name of the Lord Jesus,
giving thanks to God and the Father by him.*

COLOSSIANS 3:17 KJV

What do we offer to God when we are blessed with good things? Do we even remember to say thank you? The Lord has given us so much, and we should always and everywhere give Him thanks and praise.

In bad times, please be my strength; in good times, celebrate with me, Lord. Thank You for being with me, doing so much for me, and giving so much to me. Amen.

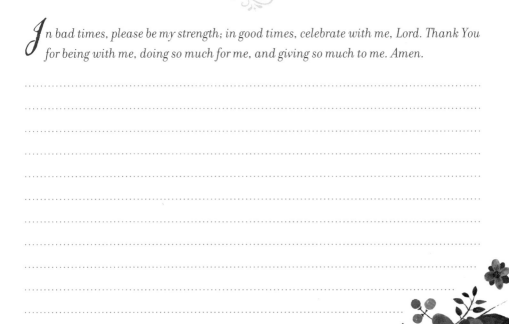

Day 346
ADVICE

Plans are established by seeking advice; so if you wage war, obtain guidance.
PROVERBS 20:18 NIV

"Now listen to me, and let me give you a word of advice, and may God be with you.
You should continue to be the people's representative before God,
bringing their disputes to him."
EXODUS 18:19 NLT

Without the counsel of the Lord, everything is ignorance. In trying to deal with our problems apart from God, we are creating more problems than we can handle. The answer is not in running from the Lord, but in running to Him.

O Lord, be close to me, building me up and keeping me ever in Your loving care. Amen.

The violence of the wicked will destroy them, because they refuse to do what is right.

PROVERBS 21:7 NCV

Do not be afraid of sudden terror or of the ruin of the wicked, when it comes.

PROVERBS 3:25 ESV

Terrible things are done all around us. We must hold on to God's goodness and His strength so we can endure such inconceivable crimes. Our Lord is greater than anything on earth. His will be done!

*L*ord, while the evil days keep coming, grant me strength enough to endure until the end. *Amen.*

Day 348
HONOR

....

Honor is no more associated with fools than snow with summer or rain with harvest.

PROVERBS 26:1 NLT

Our Father in heaven, help us to honor your name.

MATTHEW 6:9 CEV

One of the best ways we can honor our Lord is to pay attention and be careful. Other people see the way we live our lives, and if we are sloppy and sinful, we can hardly hope to make others see the benefits of honoring God with their own lives.

M ake me a good example, Lord, of a life made new through Your love. I desire to honor You all my days. Amen.

....
....
....
....
....
....
....
....
....
....
....
....
....
....

Even when there was no reason for hope, Abraham kept hoping—believing that he would become the father of many nations. For God had said to him, "That's how many descendants you will have!"

ROMANS 4:18 NLT

But I will hope continually, and will yet praise thee more and more.

PSALM 71:14 KJV

Sometimes we need a boost. God sees that, and He is ready to lift us up—to give us a new vantage point of hope. Reach up to the Lord, and He will lead you to Himself, a Rock that is higher than any problem we might have.

ick me up, Lord, and hold me in Your loving arms. Inspire me with the hope only You can bring. Amen.

Day 350
PRIDE

Surely God will not hear vanity, neither will the Almighty regard it.

JOB 35:13 KJV

Pride goes before destruction, a haughty spirit before a fall.

PROVERBS 16:18 NIV

Humility is the antithesis of pride. Jesus is the perfect example of humility—putting others above self. Although He was God, He humbled Himself and became obedient to His heavenly Father by dying on the cross.

Dear Lord, convict me of any prideful spirit within me and teach me humility. Amen.

REFLECTING CHRIST

"Anyone working and living in truth and reality welcomes God-light so the work can be seen for the God-work it is."

JOHN 3:21 MSG

Just as water mirrors your face, so your face mirrors your heart.

PROVERBS 27:19 MSG

One of the greatest sins we can ever commit is to call ourselves Christians, then act in ways that are unacceptable in the sight of the Lord. We must devote ourselves to imitating Christ in all ways possible.

I pray that I might learn to walk carefully in the steps of Jesus Christ, almighty Father. Grant that I might show honor to Your truth in all ways. Amen.

Day 352
INFERTILITY

- -

*"Worship the Lord your God, and his blessing will be on your food and water.
I will take away sickness from among you, and none will miscarry
or be barren in your land. I will give you a full life span."*

Exodus 23:25–26 NIV

*Isaac prayed to the Lord on behalf of his wife, because she was barren;
and the Lord answered him and Rebekah his wife conceived.*

Genesis 25:21 NASB

Some couples who would like to have children never do. That does not mean God is
punishing them. He simply has another plan for their lives.

*Father, when I see those struggling with infertility, pour out Your compassion through
me. May I be an encouragement in their pain. Amen.*

- -
- -
- -
- -
- -
- -
- -
- -
- -
- -
- -

. . . .

"I know, my God, that you test the heart and are pleased with integrity. All these things I have given willingly and with honest intent. And now I have seen with joy how willingly your people who are here have given to you."

1 CHRONICLES 29:17 NIV

May integrity and honesty protect me, for I put my hope in you.

PSALM 25:21 NLT

Just as faith is not simply an outward thing, integrity shows what a person is from the inside out. What we really believe on the inside shows in our thoughts and actions. But all our efforts at integrity cannot earn us God's favor. Sometimes He simply pours out His favor on us, despite our failings.

Father, lead me in integrity. I want to be a witness for You from the inside out. Amen.

. . . .

Day 354
JOY

"Ask, using my name, and you will receive, and you will have abundant joy."

JOHN 16:24 NLT

But the fruit of the Spirit is. . .joy.

GALATIANS 5:22 NKJV

The saying goes, misery loves company. Miserable people spread their misery around. On the other hand, people who possess joy can also share it.

My Lord, You have filled my heart with Your love. Whenever I see sadness, let me try to meet it with a measure of Your joy. Amen.

And God has placed in the church first of all apostles, second prophets, third teachers, then miracles, then gifts of healing, of helping, of guidance, and of different kinds of tongues.

1 Corinthians 12:28 niv

Therefore it says, "When he ascended on high he led a host of captives, and he gave gifts to men."

Ephesians 4:8 esv

We have been given many wonderful gifts and talents. When we affirm the talents we have been given, then God will surely bless us, and we will be a sign to others of His goodness.

Teach me to use the gifts I have been given, Lord. Be patient with me, and touch me with Your touch of peace and grace. Amen.

. . . .

. . . .

. . . .

. . . .

. . . .

. . . .

. . . .

. . . .

. . . .

. . . .

. . . .

. . . .

Day 356
JUSTICE

The Lord loves righteousness and justice; the earth is full of his unfailing love.

Psalm 33:5 NIV

How blessed are those who keep justice, who practice righteousness at all times!

Psalm 106:3 NASB

So often it seems like the evil doers will inherit the earth, rather than the meek. Bad people with evil intentions appear blessed in many ways that good people are not. It is a hard lesson to learn that the rain falls on the just and the unjust alike.

Help me to be patient and to turn from bitter feelings toward those who do wrong, Lord. May I always remember that Your will is perfect. Amen.

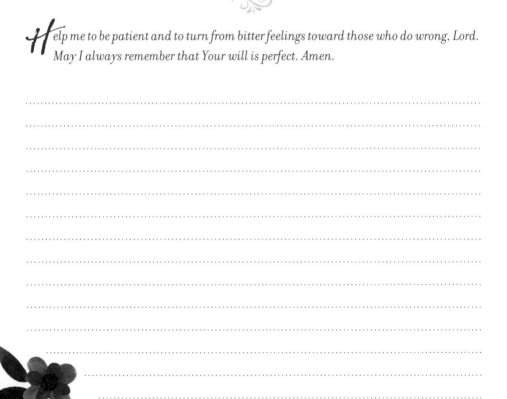

SHARING THE GOSPEL

*But even if we, or an angel from heaven, should preach to you a gospel contrary
to what we have preached to you, he is to be accursed!*

GALATIANS 1:8 NASB

*God has seen how I never stop praying for you, while I serve him with all
my heart and tell the good news about his Son.*

ROMANS 1:9 CEV

The Lord wants us to know Him completely and share our faith with all those we meet.
Hear what the Lord has to say, and proclaim it with your mouth and with your actions.

Speak through us when we have the opportunity to share Your good news, Lord. Amen.

Day 358
MARRIAGE

· ·

In God's plan women need men and men need women.

1 CORINTHIANS 11:11 NLV

Do not be unequally yoked together with unbelievers. For what fellowship has righteousness with lawlessness? And what communion has light with darkness?

2 CORINTHIANS 6:14 NKJV

Marriage is a picture of the relationship between God and His people. So, not surprisingly, God bans marriage between believers and those who have no faith in Him.

L ord, when our hearts are blind, remind us of Your loving commands. They are meant for our good. Amen.

*Therefore God has mercy on whom he wants to have mercy,
and he hardens whom he wants to harden.*

Romans 9:18 niv

Blessed are the merciful: for they shall obtain mercy.

Matthew 5:7 kjv

As we draw near to God in faith, our understanding of His mercy grows. We recognize our own deep need for Him in every corner of our lives, and we begin to respond to His love by living mercifully with others.

L ord God, left to myself, I am engulfed by sin. But You mercifully sent Your Son to die for my every wrong thought and deed. Thank You! Amen.

....

....

....

....

....

....

....

....

....

....

....

....

....

Day 360
MIRACLES

I will meditate on your majestic, glorious splendor and your wonderful miracles.

PSALM 145:5 NLT

So then, does He who provides you with the Spirit and works miracles among you,
do it by the works of the Law, or by hearing with faith?

GALATIANS 3:5 NASB

A miracle is a miracle is a miracle. The how is not nearly as important as the fact that it did happen. Our God is a God of miracles and wonders. Praise Him for what He does rather than how He does it, and you will find your faith grows by leaps and bounds.

W hen Your miracles get reduced to topics of debate, I find I lose interest, Father. Refresh me with the strangeness and awe of Your power, Lord. Amen.

Honor the LORD with your wealth, with the firstfruits of all your crops;
then your barns will be filled to overflowing.

PROVERBS 3:9–10 NIV

Command those who are rich in this present age not to be haughty, nor to trust
in uncertain riches but in the living God, who gives us richly all things to enjoy.
Let them do good, that they be rich in good works, ready to give, willing to share.

1 TIMOTHY 6:17–18 NKJV

Not only does God give us money, but He also gives the promise that He will always provide for us. That doesn't mean we can spend wildly, but as we follow Him, we will not lack what we need.

L ord, help me to use Your money wisely, and to always remember that You will provide. Amen.

Day 362
OBEDIENCE

....

And his affection for you is even greater, as he remembers the obedience of you all,
how you received him with fear and trembling.

2 Corinthians 7:15 esv

Children, obey your parents in the Lord, for this is right.

Ephesians 6:1 niv

If we learn to be obedient to the will of God, we will find that life becomes a little easier to live, and a lot more fulfilling. Life ceases to be such a struggle, and it becomes a joy.

D ear God, life can be so difficult, and I know I cannot handle everything on my own. Be with me, guiding me and helping me to follow Your commandments. Amen.

....
....
....
....
....
....
....
....
....
....
....
....

FALSE TEACHING

You have already won a big victory over those false teachers, for the Spirit in you is far stronger than anything in the world. . . . The person who has nothing to do with God will, of course, not listen to us. This is another test for telling the Spirit of Truth from the spirit of deception.

1 JOHN 4:4, 6 MSG

Someday a prophet may come along who is able to perform miracles or tell what will happen in the future. Then the prophet may say, "Let's start worshiping some new gods— some gods that we know nothing about." If the prophet says this, don't listen!

DEUTERONOMY 13:1–3 CEV

There is no substitute for the truth and saving power of Jesus Christ. Other groups and sects may appear to be sincere and good, but they attempt to lure us from what is right and good to things we should avoid.

There is so much that looks good to me, Father. Protect me from the things that would lead me far from You. Amen.

Day 364
PATIENCE

Through patience a ruler can be persuaded, and a gentle tongue can break a bone.

PROVERBS 25:15 NIV

God's Spirit makes us loving, happy, peaceful, patient.

GALATIANS 5:22 CEV

Patience is a difficult virtue to obtain, but its rewards are greater than we can begin to comprehend. Shortcuts may look promising, but it is the person who learns the benefits of waiting who is on the road to true wisdom.

Keep my feet on the right path, O Lord. Keep me from straying onto roads that seem to be easier to travel but lead nowhere. Amen.

Finally, brothers, rejoice. Aim for restoration, comfort one another,
agree with one another, live in peace; and the God of love and peace will be with you.

2 Corinthians 13:11 esv

And let the peace that comes from Christ rule in your hearts.
For as members of one body you are called to live in peace.

Colossians 3:15 nlt

Our mission in this world is to spread the peace of Christ wherever we go. As we spread peace, we find comfort in facing the future, and we come to know the peace that passes all understanding: God's own peace.

Make me an instrument of Thy peace, O Lord. Where I find discord, let me bring harmony. Where there is hatred, bring love. Amen.

Read Through the Bible in a Year

1-Jan	Gen. 1-2	Matt. 1	Ps. 1
2-Jan	Gen. 3-4	Matt. 2	Ps. 2
3-Jan	Gen. 5-7	Matt. 3	Ps. 3
4-Jan	Gen. 8-10	Matt. 4	Ps. 4
5-Jan	Gen. 11-13	Matt. 5:1-20	Ps. 5
6-Jan	Gen. 14-16	Matt. 5:21-48	Ps. 6
7-Jan	Gen. 17-18	Matt. 6:1-18	Ps. 7
8-Jan	Gen. 19-20	Matt. 6:19-34	Ps. 8
9-Jan	Gen. 21-23	Matt. 7:1-11	Ps. 9:1-8
10-Jan	Gen. 24	Matt. 7:12-29	Ps. 9:9-20
11-Jan	Gen. 25-26	Matt. 8:1-17	Ps. 10:1-11
12-Jan	Gen. 27:1-28:9	Matt. 8:18-34	Ps. 10:12-18
13-Jan	Gen. 28:10-29:35	Matt. 9	Ps. 11
14-Jan	Gen. 30:1-31:21	Matt. 10:1-15	Ps. 12
15-Jan	Gen. 31:22-32:21	Matt. 10:16-36	Ps. 13
16-Jan	Gen. 32:22-34:31	Matt. 10:37-11:6	Ps. 14
17-Jan	Gen. 35-36	Matt. 11:7-24	Ps. 15
18-Jan	Gen. 37-38	Matt. 11:25-30	Ps. 16
19-Jan	Gen. 39-40	Matt. 12:1-29	Ps. 17
20-Jan	Gen. 41	Matt. 12:30-50	Ps. 18:1-15
21-Jan	Gen. 42-43	Matt. 13:1-9	Ps. 18:16-29
22-Jan	Gen. 44-45	Matt. 13:10-23	Ps. 18:30-50
23-Jan	Gen. 46:1-47:26	Matt. 13:24-43	Ps. 19
24-Jan	Gen. 47:27-49:28	Matt. 13:44-58	Ps. 20
25-Jan	Gen. 49:29-Exod. 1:22	Matt. 14	Ps. 21
26-Jan	Exod. 2-3	Matt. 15:1-28	Ps. 22:1-21
27-Jan	Exod. 4:1-5:21	Matt. 15:29-16:12	Ps. 22:22-31
28-Jan	Exod. 5:22-7:24	Matt. 16:13-28	Ps. 23
29-Jan	Exod. 7:25-9:35	Matt. 17:1-9	Ps. 24
30-Jan	Exod. 10-11	Matt. 17:10-27	Ps. 25
31-Jan	Exod. 12	Matt. 18:1-20	Ps. 26
1-Feb	Exod. 13-14	Matt. 18:21-35	Ps. 27
2-Feb	Exod. 15-16	Matt. 19:1-15	Ps. 28
3-Feb	Exod. 17-19	Matt. 19:16-30	Ps. 29
4-Feb	Exod. 20-21	Matt. 20:1-19	Ps. 30
5-Feb	Exod. 22-23	Matt. 20:20-34	Ps. 31:1-8
6-Feb	Exod. 24-25	Matt. 21:1-27	Ps. 31:9-18
7-Feb	Exod 26-27	Matt. 21:28-46	Ps. 31:19-24
8-Feb	Exod. 28	Matt. 22	Ps. 32
9-Feb	Exod. 29	Matt. 23:1-36	Ps. 33:1-12
10-Feb	Exod. 30-31	Matt. 23:37-24:28	Ps. 33:13-22
11-Feb	Exod. 32-33	Matt. 24:29-51	Ps. 34:1-7

12-Feb	Exod. 34:1-35:29	Matt. 25:1-13	Ps. 34:8-22
13-Feb	Exod. 35:30-37:29	Matt. 25:14-30	Ps. 35:1-8
14-Feb	Exod. 38-39	Matt. 25:31-46	Ps. 35:9-17
15-Feb	Exod. 40	Matt. 26:1-35	Ps. 35:18-28
16-Feb	Lev. 1-3	Matt. 26:36-68	Ps. 36:1-6
17-Feb	Lev. 4:1-5:13	Matt. 26:69-27:26	Ps. 36:7-12
18-Feb	Lev. 5:14 -7:21	Matt. 27:27-50	Ps. 37:1-6
19-Feb	Lev. 7:22-8:36	Matt. 27:51-66	Ps. 37:7-26
20-Feb	Lev. 9-10	Matt. 28	Ps. 37:27-40
21-Feb	Lev. 11-12	Mark 1:1-28	Ps. 38
22-Feb	Lev. 13	Mark 1:29-39	Ps. 39
23-Feb	Lev. 14	Mark 1:40-2:12	Ps. 40:1-8
24-Feb	Lev. 15	Mark 2:13-3:35	Ps. 40:9-17
25-Feb	Lev. 16-17	Mark 4:1-20	Ps. 41:1-4
26-Feb	Lev. 18-19	Mark 4:21-41	Ps. 41:5-13
27-Feb	Lev. 20	Mark 5	Ps. 42-43
28-Feb	Lev. 21-22	Mark 6:1-13	Ps. 44
1-Mar	Lev. 23-24	Mark 6:14-29	Ps. 45:1-5
2-Mar	Lev. 25	Mark 6:30-56	Ps. 45:6-12
3-Mar	Lev. 26	Mark 7	Ps. 45:13-17
4-Mar	Lev. 27	Mark 8	Ps. 46
5-Mar	Num. 1-2	Mark 9:1-13	Ps. 47
6-Mar	Num. 3	Mark 9:14-50	Ps. 48:1-8
7-Mar	Num. 4	Mark 10:1-34	Ps. 48:9-14
8-Mar	Num. 5:1-6:21	Mark 10:35-52	Ps. 49:1-9
9-Mar	Num. 6:22-7:47	Mark 11	Ps. 49:10-20
10-Mar	Num. 7:48-8:4	Mark 12:1-27	Ps. 50:1-15
11-Mar	Num. 8:5-9:23	Mark 12:28-44	Ps. 50:16-23
12-Mar	Num. 10-11	Mark 13:1-8	Ps. 51:1-9
13-Mar	Num. 12-13	Mark 13:9-37	Ps. 51:10-19
14-Mar	Num. 14	Mark 14:1-31	Ps. 52
15-Mar	Num. 15	Mark 14:32-72	Ps. 53
16-Mar	Num. 16	Mark 15:1-32	Ps. 54
17-Mar	Num. 17-18	Mark 15:33-47	Ps. 55
18-Mar	Num. 19-20	Mark 16	Ps. 56:1-7
19-Mar	Num. 21:1-22:20	Luke 1:1-25	Ps. 56:8-13
20-Mar	Num. 22:21-23:30	Luke 1:26-56	Ps. 57
21-Mar	Num. 24-25	Luke 1:57-2:20	Ps. 58
22-Mar	Num. 26:1-27:11	Luke 2:21-38	Ps. 59:1-8
23-Mar	Num. 27:12-29:11	Luke 2:39-52	Ps. 59:9-17
24-Mar	Num. 29:12-30:16	Luke 3	Ps. 60:1-5
25-Mar	Num. 31	Luke 4	Ps. 60:6-12
26-Mar	Num. 32-33	Luke 5:1-16	Ps. 61
27-Mar	Num. 34-36	Luke 5:17-32	Ps. 62:1-6
28-Mar	Deut. 1:1-2:25	Luke 5:33-6:11	Ps. 62:7-12
29-Mar	Deut. 2:26-4:14	Luke 6:12-35	Ps. 63:1-5
30-Mar	Deut. 4:15-5:22	Luke 6:36-49	Ps. 63:6-11

31-Mar	Deut. 5:23-7:26	Luke 7:1-17	Ps. 64:1-5
1-Apr	Deut. 8-9	Luke 7:18-35	Ps. 64:6-10
2-Apr	Deut. 10-11	Luke 7:36-8:3	Ps. 65:1-8
3-Apr	Deut. 12-13	Luke 8:4-21	Ps. 65:9-13
4-Apr	Deut. 14:1-16:8	Luke 8:22-39	Ps. 66:1-7
5-Apr	Deut. 16:9-18:22	Luke 8:40-56	Ps. 66:8-15
6-Apr	Deut. 19:1-21:9	Luke 9:1-22	Ps. 66:16-20
7-Apr	Deut. 21:10-23:8	Luke 9:23-42	Ps. 67
8-Apr	Deut. 23:9-25:19	Luke 9:43-62	Ps. 68:1-6
9-Apr	Deut. 26:1-28:14	Luke 10:1-20	Ps. 68:7-14
10-Apr	Deut. 28:15-68	Luke 10:21-37	Ps. 68:15-19
11-Apr	Deut. 29-30	Luke 10:38-11:23	Ps. 68:20-27
12-Apr	Deut. 31:1-32:22	Luke 11:24-36	Ps. 68:28-35
13-Apr	Deut. 32:23-33:29	Luke 11:37-54	Ps. 69:1-9
14-Apr	Deut. 34-Josh. 2	Luke 12:1-15	Ps. 69:10-17
15-Apr	Josh. 3:1-5:12	Luke 12:16-40	Ps. 69:18-28
16-Apr	Josh. 5:13-7:26	Luke 12:41-48	Ps. 69:29-36
17-Apr	Josh. 8-9	Luke 12:49-59	Ps. 70
18-Apr	Josh. 10:1-11:15	Luke 13:1-21	Ps. 71:1-6
19-Apr	Josh. 11:16-13:33	Luke 13:22-35	Ps. 71:7-16
20-Apr	Josh. 14-16	Luke 14:1-15	Ps. 71:17-21
21-Apr	Josh. 17:1-19:16	Luke 14:16-35	Ps. 71:22-24
22-Apr	Josh. 19:17-21:42	Luke 15:1-10	Ps. 72:1-11
23-Apr	Josh. 21:43-22:34	Luke 15:11-32	Ps. 72:12-20
24-Apr	Josh. 23-24	Luke 16:1-18	Ps. 73:1-9
25-Apr	Judg. 1-2	Luke 16:19-17:10	Ps. 73:10-20
26-Apr	Judg. 3-4	Luke 17:11-37	Ps. 73:21-28
27-Apr	Judg. 5:1-6:24	Luke 18:1-17	Ps. 74:1-3
28-Apr	Judg. 6:25-7:25	Luke 18:18-43	Ps. 74:4-11
29-Apr	Judg. 8:1-9:23	Luke 19:1-28	Ps. 74:12-17
30-Apr	Judg. 9:24-10:18	Luke 19:29-48	Ps. 74:18-23
1-May	Judg. 11:1-12:7	Luke 20:1-26	Ps. 75:1-7
2-May	Judg. 12:8-14:20	Luke 20:27-47	Ps. 75:8-10
3-May	Judg. 15-16	Luke 21:1-19	Ps. 76:1-7
4-May	Judg. 17-18	Luke 21:20-22:6	Ps. 76:8-12
5-May	Judg. 19:1-20:23	Luke 22:7-30	Ps. 77:1-11
6-May	Judg. 20:24-21:25	Luke 22:31-54	Ps. 77:12-20
7-May	Ruth 1-2	Luke 22:55-23:25	Ps. 78:1-4
8-May	Ruth 3-4	Luke 23:26-24:12	Ps. 78:5-8
9-May	1 Sam. 1:1-2:21	Luke 24:13-53	Ps. 78:9-16
10-May	1 Sam. 2:22-4:22	John 1:1-28	Ps. 78:17-24
11-May	1 Sam. 5-7	John 1:29-51	Ps. 78:25-33
12-May	1 Sam. 8:1-9:26	John 2	Ps. 78:34-41
13-May	1 Sam. 9:27-11:15	John 3:1-22	Ps. 78:42-55
14-May	1 Sam. 12-13	John 3:23-4:10	Ps. 78:56-66
15-May	1 Sam. 14	John 4:11-38	Ps. 78:67-72
16-May	1 Sam. 15-16	John 4:39-54	Ps. 79:1-7

17-May	1 Sam. 17	John 5:1-24	Ps. 79:8-13
18-May	1 Sam. 18-19	John 5:25-47	Ps. 80:1-7
19-May	1 Sam. 20-21	John 6:1-21	Ps. 80:8-19
20-May	1 Sam. 22-23	John 6:22-42	Ps. 81:1-10
21-May	1 Sam. 24:1-25:31	John 6:43-71	Ps. 81:11-16
22-May	1 Sam. 25:32-27:12	John 7:1-24	Ps. 82
23-May	1 Sam. 28-29	John 7:25-8:11	Ps. 83
24-May	1 Sam. 30-31	John 8:12-47	Ps. 84:1-4
25-May	2 Sam. 1-2	John 8:48-9:12	Ps. 84:5-12
26-May	2 Sam. 3-4	John 9:13-34	Ps. 85:1-7
27-May	2 Sam. 5:1-7:17	John 9:35-10:10	Ps. 85:8-13
28-May	2 Sam. 7:18-10:19	John 10:11-30	Ps. 86:1-10
29-May	2 Sam. 11:1-12:25	John 10:31-11:16	Ps. 86:11-17
30-May	2 Sam. 12:26-13:39	John 11:17-54	Ps. 87
31-May	2 Sam. 14:1-15:12	John 11:55-12:19	Ps. 88:1-9
1-Jun	2 Sam. 15:13-16:23	John 12:20-43	Ps. 88:10-18
2-Jun	2 Sam. 17:1-18:18	John 12:44-13:20	Ps. 89:1-6
3-Jun	2 Sam. 18:19-19:39	John 13:21-38	Ps. 89:7-13
4-Jun	2 Sam. 19:40-21:22	John 14:1-17	Ps. 89:14-18
5-Jun	2 Sam. 22:1-23:7	John 14:18-15:27	Ps. 89:19-29
6-Jun	2 Sam. 23:8-24:25	John 16:1-22	Ps. 89:30-37
7-Jun	1 Kings 1	John 16:23-17:5	Ps. 89:38-52
8-Jun	1 Kings 2	John 17:6-26	Ps. 90:1-12
9-Jun	1 Kings 3-4	John 18:1-27	Ps. 90:13-17
10-Jun	1 Kings 5-6	John 18:28-19:5	Ps. 91:1-10
11-Jun	1 Kings 7	John 19:6-25a	Ps. 91:11-16
12-Jun	1 Kings 8:1-53	John 19:25b-42	Ps. 92:1-9
13-Jun	1 Kings 8:54-10:13	John 20:1-18	Ps. 92:10-15
14-Jun	1 Kings 10:14-11:43	John 20:19-31	Ps. 93
15-Jun	1 Kings 12:1-13:10	John 21	Ps. 94:1-11
16-Jun	1 Kings 13:11-14:31	Acts 1:1-11	Ps. 94:12-23
17-Jun	1 Kings 15:1-16:20	Acts 1:12-26	Ps. 95
18-Jun	1 Kings 16:21-18:19	Acts 2:1-21	Ps. 96:1-8
19-Jun	1 Kings 18:20-19:21	Acts 2:22-41	Ps. 96:9-13
20-Jun	1 Kings 20	Acts 2:42-3:26	Ps. 97:1-6
21-Jun	1 Kings 21:1-22:28	Acts 4:1-22	Ps. 97:7-12
22-Jun	1 Kings 22:29- 2 Kings 1:18	Acts 4:23-5:11	Ps. 98
23-Jun	2 Kings 2-3	Acts 5:12-28	Ps. 99
24-Jun	2 Kings 4	Acts 5:29-6:15	Ps. 100
25-Jun	2 Kings 5:1-6:23	Acts 7:1-16	Ps. 101
26-Jun	2 Kings 6:24-8:15	Acts 7:17-36	Ps. 102:1-7
27-Jun	2 Kings 8:16-9:37	Acts 7:37-53	Ps. 102:8-17
28-Jun	2 Kings 10-11	Acts 7:54-8:8	Ps. 102:18-28
29-Jun	2 Kings 12-13	Acts 8:9-40	Ps. 103:1-9
30-Jun	2 Kings 14-15	Acts 9:1-16	Ps. 103:10-14
1-Jul	2 Kings 16-17	Acts 9:17-31	Ps. 103:15-22

2-Jul	2 Kings 18:1-19:7	Acts 9:32-10:16	Ps. 104:1-9
3-Jul	2 Kings 19:8-20:21	Acts 10:17-33	Ps. 104:10-23
4-Jul	2 Kings 21:1-22:20	Acts 10:34-11:18	Ps. 104: 24-30
5-Jul	2 Kings 23	Acts 11:19-12:17	Ps. 104:31-35
6-Jul	2 Kings 24-25	Acts 12:18-13:13	Ps. 105:1-7
7-Jul	1 Chron. 1-2	Acts 13:14-43	Ps. 105:8-15
8-Jul	1 Chron. 3:1-5:10	Acts 13:44-14:10	Ps. 105:16-28
9-Jul	1 Chron. 5:11-6:81	Acts 14:11-28	Ps. 105:29-36
10-Jul	1 Chron. 7:1-9:9	Acts 15:1-18	Ps. 105:37-45
11-Jul	1 Chron. 9:10-11:9	Acts 15:19-41	Ps. 106:1-12
12-Jul	1 Chron. 11:10-12:40	Acts 16:1-15	Ps. 106:13-27
13-Jul	1 Chron. 13-15	Acts 16:16-40	Ps. 106:28-33
14-Jul	1 Chron. 16-17	Acts 17:1-14	Ps. 106:34-43
15-Jul	1 Chron. 18-20	Acts 17:15-34	Ps. 106:44-48
16-Jul	1 Chron. 21-22	Acts 18:1-23	Ps. 107:1-9
17-Jul	1 Chron. 23-25	Acts 18:24-19:10	Ps. 107:10-16
18-Jul	1 Chron. 26-27	Acts 19:11-22	Ps. 107:17-32
19-Jul	1 Chron. 28-29	Acts 19:23-41	Ps. 107:33-38
20-Jul	2 Chron. 1-3	Acts 20:1-16	Ps. 107:39-43
21-Jul	2 Chron. 4:1-6:11	Acts 20:17-38	Ps. 108
22-Jul	2 Chron. 6:12-7:10	Acts 21:1-14	Ps. 109:1-20
23-Jul	2 Chron. 7:11-9:28	Acts 21:15-32	Ps. 109:21-31
24-Jul	2 Chron. 9:29-12:16	Acts 21:33-22:16	Ps. 110:1-3
25-Jul	2 Chron. 13-15	Acts 22:17-23:11	Ps. 110:4-7
26-Jul	2 Chron. 16-17	Acts 23:12-24:21	Ps. 111
27-Jul	2 Chron. 18-19	Acts 24:22-25:12	Ps. 112
28-Jul	2 Chron. 20-21	Acts 25:13-27	Ps. 113
29-Jul	2 Chron. 22-23	Acts 26	Ps. 114
30-Jul	2 Chron. 24:1-25:16	Acts 27:1-20	Ps. 115:1-10
31-Jul	2 Chron. 25:17-27:9	Acts 27:21-28:6	Ps. 115:11-18
1-Aug	2 Chron. 28:1-29:19	Acts 28:7-31	Ps. 116:1-5
2-Aug	2 Chron. 29:20-30:27	Rom. 1:1-17	Ps. 116:6-19
3-Aug	2 Chron. 31-32	Rom. 1:18-32	Ps. 117
4-Aug	2 Chron. 33:1-34:7	Rom. 2	Ps. 118:1-18
5-Aug	2 Chron. 34:8-35:19	Rom. 3:1-26	Ps. 118:19-23
6-Aug	2 Chron. 35:20-36:23	Rom. 3:27-4:25	Ps. 118:24-29
7-Aug	Ezra 1-3	Rom. 5	Ps. 119:1-8
8-Aug	Ezra 4-5	Rom. 6:1-7:6	Ps. 119:9-16
9-Aug	Ezra 6:1-7:26	Rom. 7:7-25	Ps. 119:17-32
10-Aug	Ezra 7:27-9:4	Rom. 8:1-27	Ps. 119:33-40
11-Aug	Ezra 9:5-10:44	Rom. 8:28-39	Ps. 119:41-64
12-Aug	Neh. 1:1-3:16	Rom. 9:1-18	Ps. 119:65-72
13-Aug	Neh. 3:17-5:13	Rom. 9:19-33	Ps. 119:73-80
14-Aug	Neh. 5:14-7:73	Rom. 10:1-13	Ps. 119:81-88
15-Aug	Neh. 8:1-9:5	Rom. 10:14-11:24	Ps. 119:89-104
16-Aug	Neh. 9:6-10:27	Rom. 11:25-12:8	Ps. 119:105-120
17-Aug	Neh. 10:28-12:26	Rom. 12:9-13:7	Ps. 119:121-128

18-Aug	Neh. 12:27-13:31	Rom. 13:8-14:12	Ps. 119:129-136
19-Aug	Esther 1:1-2:18	Rom. 14:13-15:13	Ps. 119:137-152
20-Aug	Esther 2:19-5:14	Rom. 15:14-21	Ps. 119:153-168
21-Aug	Esther. 6-8	Rom. 15:22-33	Ps. 119:169-176
22-Aug	Esther 9-10	Rom. 16	Ps. 120-122
23-Aug	Job 1-3	1 Cor. 1:1-25	Ps. 123
24-Aug	Job 4-6	1 Cor. 1:26-2:16	Ps. 124-125
25-Aug	Job 7-9	1 Cor. 3	Ps. 126-127
26-Aug	Job 10-13	1 Cor. 4:1-13	Ps. 128-129
27-Aug	Job 14-16	1 Cor. 4:14-5:13	Ps. 130
28-Aug	Job 17-20	1 Cor. 6	Ps. 131
29-Aug	Job 21-23	1 Cor. 7:1-16	Ps. 132
30-Aug	Job 24-27	1 Cor. 7:17-40	Ps. 133-134
31-Aug	Job 28-30	1 Cor. 8	Ps. 135
1-Sep	Job 31-33	1 Cor. 9:1-18	Ps. 136:1-9
2-Sep	Job 34-36	1 Cor. 9:19-10:13	Ps. 136:10-26
3-Sep	Job 37-39	1 Cor. 10:14-11:1	Ps. 137
4-Sep	Job 40-42	1 Cor. 11:2-34	Ps. 138
5-Sep	Eccles. 1:1-3:15	1 Cor. 12:1-26	Ps. 139:1-6
6-Sep	Eccles. 3:16-6:12	1 Cor. 12:27-13:13	Ps. 139:7-18
7-Sep	Eccles. 7:1-9:12	1 Cor. 14:1-22	Ps. 139:19-24
8-Sep	Eccles. 9:13-12:14	1 Cor. 14:23-15:11	Ps. 140:1-8
9-Sep	SS 1-4	1 Cor. 15:12-34	Ps. 140:9-13
10-Sep	SS 5-8	1 Cor. 15:35-58	Ps. 141
11-Sep	Isa. 1-2	1 Cor. 16	Ps. 142
12-Sep	Isa. 3-5	2 Cor. 1:1-11	Ps. 143:1-6
13-Sep	Isa. 6-8	2 Cor. 1:12-2:4	Ps. 143:7-12
14-Sep	Isa. 9-10	2 Cor. 2:5-17	Ps. 144
15-Sep	Isa. 11-13	2 Cor. 3	Ps. 145
16-Sep	Isa. 14-16	2 Cor. 4	Ps. 146
17-Sep	Isa. 17-19	2 Cor. 5	Ps. 147:1-11
18-Sep	Isa. 20-23	2 Cor. 6	Ps. 147:12-20
19-Sep	Isa. 24:1-26:19	2 Cor. 7	Ps. 148
20-Sep	Isa. 26:20-28:29	2 Cor. 8	Ps. 149-150
21-Sep	Isa. 29-30	2 Cor. 9	Prov. 1:1-9
22-Sep	Isa. 31-33	2 Cor. 10	Prov. 1:10-22
23-Sep	Isa. 34-36	2 Cor. 11	Prov. 1:23-26
24-Sep	Isa. 37-38	2 Cor. 12:1-10	Prov. 1:27-33
25-Sep	Isa. 39-40	2 Cor. 12:11-13:14	Prov. 2:1-15
26-Sep	Isa. 41-42	Gal. 1	Prov. 2:16-22
27-Sep	Isa. 43:1-44:20	Gal. 2	Prov. 3:1-12
28-Sep	Isa. 44:21-46:13	Gal. 3:1-18	Prov. 3:13-26
29-Sep	Isa. 47:1-49:13	Gal 3:19-29	Prov. 3:27-35
30-Sep	Isa. 49:14-51:23	Gal 4:1-11	Prov. 4:1-19
1-Oct	Isa. 52-54	Gal. 4:12-31	Prov. 4:20-27
2-Oct	Isa. 55-57	Gal. 5	Prov. 5:1-14
3-Oct	Isa. 58-59	Gal. 6	Prov. 5:15-23

4-Oct	Isa. 60-62	Eph. 1	Prov. 6:1-5
5-Oct	Isa. 63:1-65:16	Eph. 2	Prov. 6:6-19
6-Oct	Isa. 65:17-66:24	Eph. 3:1-4:16	Prov. 6:20-26
7-Oct	Jer. 1-2	Eph. 4:17-32	Prov. 6:27-35
8-Oct	Jer. 3:1-4:22	Eph. 5	Prov. 7:1-5
9-Oct	Jer. 4:23-5:31	Eph. 6	Prov. 7:6-27
10-Oct	Jer. 6:1-7:26	Phil. 1:1-26	Prov. 8:1-11
11-Oct	Jer. 7:26-9:16	Phil. 1:27-2:18	Prov. 8:12-21
12-Oct	Jer. 9:17-11:17	Phil 2:19-30	Prov. 8:22-36
13-Oct	Jer. 11:18-13:27	Phil. 3	Prov. 9:1-6
14-Oct	Jer. 14-15	Phil. 4	Prov. 9:7-18
15-Oct	Jer. 16-17	Col. 1:1-23	Prov. 10:1-5
16-Oct	Jer. 18:1-20:6	Col. 1:24-2:15	Prov. 10:6-14
17-Oct	Jer. 20:7-22:19	Col. 2:16-3:4	Prov. 10:15-26
18-Oct	Jer. 22:20-23:40	Col. 3:5-4:1	Prov. 10:27-32
19-Oct	Jer. 24-25	Col. 4:2-18	Prov. 11:1-11
20-Oct	Jer. 26-27	1 Thes. 1:1-2:8	Prov. 11:12-21
21-Oct	Jer. 28-29	1 Thes. 2:9-3:13	Prov. 11:22-26
22-Oct	Jer. 30:1-31:22	1 Thes. 4:1-5:11	Prov. 11:27-31
23-Oct	Jer. 31:23-32:35	1 Thes. 5:12-28	Prov. 12:1-14
24-Oct	Jer. 32:36-34:7	2 Thes. 1-2	Prov. 12:15-20
25-Oct	Jer. 34:8-36:10	2 Thes. 3	Prov. 12:21-28
26-Oct	Jer. 36:11-38:13	1 Tim. 1:1-17	Prov. 13:1-4
27-Oct	Jer. 38:14-40:6	1 Tim. 1:18-3:13	Prov. 13:5-13
28-Oct	Jer. 40:7-42:22	1 Tim. 3:14-4:10	Prov. 13:14-21
29-Oct	Jer. 43-44	1 Tim. 4:11-5:16	Prov. 13:22-25
30-Oct	Jer. 45-47	1 Tim. 5:17-6:21	Prov. 14:1-6
31-Oct	Jer. 48:1-49:6	2 Tim. 1	Prov. 14:7-22
1-Nov	Jer. 49:7-50:16	2 Tim. 2	Prov. 14:23-27
2-Nov	Jer. 50:17-51:14	2 Tim. 3	Prov. 14:28-35
3-Nov	Jer. 51:15-64	2 Tim. 4	Prov. 15:1-9
4-Nov	Jer. 52-Lam. 1	Ti. 1:1-9	Prov. 15:10-17
5-Nov	Lam. 2:1-3:38	Ti. 1:10-2:15	Prov. 15:18-26
6-Nov	Lam. 3:39-5:22	Ti. 3	Prov. 15:27-33
7-Nov	Ezek. 1:1-3:21	Philemon 1	Prov. 16:1-9
8-Nov	Ezek. 3:22-5:17	Heb. 1:1-2:4	Prov. 16:10-21
9-Nov	Ezek. 6-7	Heb. 2:5-18	Prov. 16:22-33
10-Nov	Ezek. 8-10	Heb. 3:1-4:3	Prov. 17:1-5
11-Nov	Ezek. 11-12	Heb. 4:4-5:10	Prov. 17:6-12
12-Nov	Ezek. 13-14	Heb. 5:11-6:20	Prov. 17:13-22
13-Nov	Ezek. 15:1-16:43	Heb. 7:1-28	Prov. 17:23-28
14-Nov	Ezek. 16:44-17:24	Heb. 8:1-9:10	Prov. 18:1-7
15-Nov	Ezek. 18-19	Heb. 9:11-28	Prov. 18:8-17
16-Nov	Ezek. 20	Heb. 10:1-25	Prov. 18:18-24
17-Nov	Ezek. 21-22	Heb. 10:26-39	Prov. 19:1-8
18-Nov	Ezek. 23	Heb. 11:1-31	Prov. 19:9-14
19-Nov	Ezek. 24-26	Heb. 11:32-40	Prov. 19:15-21

20-Nov	Ezek. 27-28	Heb. 12:1-13	Prov. 19:22-29
21-Nov	Ezek. 29-30	Heb. 12:14-29	Prov. 20:1-18
22-Nov	Ezek. 31-32	Heb. 13	Prov. 20:19-24
23-Nov	Ezek. 33:1-34:10	Jas. 1	Prov. 20:25-30
24-Nov	Ezek. 34:11-36:15	Jas. 2	Prov. 21:1-8
25-Nov	Ezek. 36:16-37:28	Jas. 3	Prov. 21:9-18
26-Nov	Ezek. 38-39	Jas. 4:1-5:6	Prov. 21:19-24
27-Nov	Ezek. 40	Jas. 5:7-20	Prov. 21:25-31
28-Nov	Ezek. 41:1-43:12	1 Pet. 1:1-12	Prov. 22:1-9
29-Nov	Ezek. 43;13-44:31	1 Pet. 1:13-2:3	Prov. 22:10-23
30-Nov	Ezek. 45-46	1 Pet. 2:4-17	Prov. 22:24-29
1-Dec	Ezek. 47-48	1 Pet. 2:18-3:7	Prov. 23:1-9
2-Dec	Dan. 1:1-2:23	1 Pet. 3:8-4:19	Prov. 23:10-16
3-Dec	Dan. 2:24-3:30	1 Pet. 5	Prov. 23:17-25
4-Dec	Dan. 4	2 Pet. 1	Prov. 23:26-35
5-Dec	Dan. 5	2 Pet. 2	Prov. 24:1-18
6-Dec	Dan. 6:1-7:14	2 Pet. 3	Prov. 24:19-27
7-Dec	Dan. 7:15-8:27	1 John 1:1-2:17	Prov. 24:28-34
8-Dec	Dan. 9-10	1 John 2:18-29	Prov. 25:1-12
9-Dec	Dan. 11-12	1 John 3:1-12	Prov. 25:13-17
10-Dec	Hos. 1-3	1 John 3:13-4:16	Prov. 25:18-28
11-Dec	Hos. 4-6	1 John 4:17-5:21	Prov. 26:1-16
12-Dec	Hos. 7-10	2 John	Prov. 26:17-21
13-Dec	Hos. 11-14	3 John	Prov. 26:22-27:9
14-Dec	Joel 1:1-2:17	Jude	Prov. 27:10-17
15-Dec	Joel 2:18-3:21	Rev. 1:1-2:11	Prov. 27:18-27
16-Dec	Amos 1:1-4:5	Rev. 2:12-29	Prov. 28:1-8
17-Dec	Amos 4:6-6:14	Rev. 3	Prov. 28:9-16
18-Dec	Amos 7-9	Rev. 4:1-5:5	Prov. 28:17-24
19-Dec	Obad-Jonah	Rev. 5:6-14	Prov. 28:25-28
20-Dec	Mic. 1:1-4:5	Rev. 6:1-7:8	Prov. 29:1-8
21-Dec	Mic. 4:6-7:20	Rev. 7:9-8:13	Prov. 29:9-14
22-Dec	Nah. 1-3	Rev. 9-10	Prov. 29:15-23
23-Dec	Hab. 1-3	Rev. 11	Prov. 29:24-27
24-Dec	Zeph. 1-3	Rev. 12	Prov. 30:1-6
25-Dec	Hag. 1-2	Rev. 13:1-14:13	Prov. 30:7-16
26-Dec	Zech. 1-4	Rev. 14:14-16:3	Prov. 30:17-20
27-Dec	Zech. 5-8	Rev. 16:4-21	Prov. 30:21-28
28-Dec	Zech. 9-11	Rev. 17:1-18:8	Prov. 30:29-33
29-Dec	Zech. 12-14	Rev. 18:9-24	Prov. 31:1-9
30-Dec	Mal. 1-2	Rev. 19-20	Prov. 31:10-17
31-Dec	Mal. 3-4	Rev. 21-22	Prov. 31:18-31

Expanded Editions of
The Bible Promise Book® Just for Women

The Bible Promise Book® for Hope and Healing

Featuring dozens of timely topics—including Addiction, Rest, Peace, Forgiveness, Eternity, God's Love, Salvation, God's Power, Prayer, Comfort, and Perseverance—readers will find hundreds of verses from God's Word that will speak to their daily needs. *The Bible Promise Book® for Hope and Healing* is ideal for personal use and for ministries.

Paperback / 978-1-63058-860-1 / $5.99

The Bible Promise Book® for Women Prayer Edition

Barbour's Bible Promise Books are perennial bestsellers with millions of copies in print. Now, The *Bible Promise Book*® is available in a paperback edition for women featuring scripture, encouraging prayers, inspiring quotes, and bonus journaling pages. With more than 60 topics and nearly 1,000 total verses, it makes a perfect gift for any occasion.

Paperback / 978-1-63409-947-9 / $9.99